Common Things That Are Suddenly Special

A Memoir by Brenda Liddy.
Inspired by Sei Shonagon's Pillow Book

By

Dr Brenda Josephine Liddy

Dr Brenda Liddy holds a PhD from the University of Ulster. She is an Early Modern scholar and her special interest is women's war drama. Dr Liddy teaches English at the Northern Regional College. She is also a published poet and author, and teaches poetry in local primary and secondary schools as part a community arts project. She teaches creative writing at The School of Education, Open Learning, Queen's University, Belfast.

She has published two academic books, which were based on her doctoral studies. *Women's War Drama in England in the Seventeenth Century* and *The Drama of War in the Theatre of Anne Devlin, Marie Jones, and Christina Reid, Three Irish Playwrights* have been well received and continue to gain critical attention.

The author lives in north Belfast and is active in community education and serves on the Board of the Black Mountain Zen Centre, a local charity which promotes meditation and lay practice.

ISBN: 1493504770
ISBN 13: 9781493504770

Contents Page

Introduction to Common Things That Are Suddenly Special by Brenda Liddy .... *xv*

Chapter One: Thing That Induce Half-Heartedness *1*
[1] The Seasons 1
[2] My Favourite Months 3
[3] I Love the New Year 3
[4] On the Third Day of the Third Month 5
[5] Spring Blossoms 6
[6] Every Day is a Good Day 6
[7] Different Ways of Speaking 8
[8] Elegant Things 9
[9] The Cat who lived in the Palace 10
[10] Mountains 14
[11] Markets 14
[12] Peaks 15
[13] Plains 16
[14] River Pools 16
[15] Bodies of Water 17
[16] Imperial Tombs 18
[17] Ferry Crossings 18
[18] Large Buildings 18
[19] Residences 19
[20] The Sliding Panels 19

[21] Women without Prospect 21
[22] Dispiriting Things 22
[23] Occasional Things That Induce Half-Heartedness 23
[24] Things That People Despise 25
[25] Infuriating Things 27

Chapter Two: Things to Make the Heart Go Faster 29
[26] Things to Make the Heart Go Faster 29
[27] Things That Make You Feel Nostalgic 31
[28] Things That Make You Feel Cheerful 36
[29] A Palm-Leaf Carriage 39
[30] A Priest Who Gives a Sermon Should be Handsome 44
[31] While I Was Visiting the Bodai Temple 46
[32] The Palace Known as Koshirakawa 46
[33] In the Seventh Month When the Heat is Dreadful 48
[34] Flowering Trees 48
[35] Ponds 51
[36] Seasonal Palace Festivals 51
[37] Trees that Have no Flowers 52
[38] Birds 52
[39] Refined and Elegant Things 54
[40] Insects 54
[41] In the Seventh Month the Wind Blows Hard 55
[42] Unsuitable Things 56
[43] A Lot of us are Gathered in the Long Room 57
[44] No Menial Position Could be Finer than that of
     Palace Groundswomen 58
[45] Amongst the Serving Men's Positions 58
[46] Secretary Controller Yukinari 58
[47] Horses 59
[48] Oxen 61
[49] Cats 61
[50] Carriage Runners 63

Chapter Three: Things that cannot be Compared 65

[51] Page Boys 65

[52] Ox Handlers 65

[53] The Mighty Roll Call 65

[54] It's Disgusting When a Well-Bred Young Man
Casually Calls Out the Name of Some Low-ranking
Woman he's Visiting 66

[55] Young People and Babies should be Plump 67

[56] Little Children Waving Quaint Toy Bows 67

[57] The Central Gate of a Grand House Lies Open 68

[58] Waterfalls 68

[59] Rivers 69

[60] I Do Wish Men, When They're Taking Their Leave
from a Lady at Dawn, Wouldn't Insist on Adjusting
their Clothes to a Nicety 69

[61] Bridges 70

[62] Villages 70

[63] Plants 70

[64] Flowering Plants 70

[65] Poetry Anthologies 71

[66] Poetic Topics 71

[67] Disturbing Things 71

[68] Things that cannot be Compared 72

[69] Summer Provides the Most Delightful Setting for a
Secret Assignation 73

[70] A Man Comes Calling, Perhaps for Some Intimate
Conversation 73

[71] Rare Things 73

[72] Our Apartments in the Long Room 73

[73] When Her Majesty Was in Residence 73

[74] Things Later Regretted 74

[75] Things that Look Enjoyable 74

[76] The Day after the Litany of Buddha Names 74
[77] When Secretary Captain Tadanobu Heard Certain
    Baseless and Ridiculous Rumours That Were
    Circulating Concerning Me 74
[78] The Following Year, Towards the End of the
    Second Month 74
[79] When One's Returned Home on a Visit. 74
[80] Things that Create the Appearance of Deep Emotion 75
[81] After Our Visit to the Guard Office 75
[82] Once When her Majesty was in Residence 75
[83] Splendid Things 76
[84] Things of Elegant Beauty 76
[85] When Her Majesty Provided the Gosechi Dancers 76
[86] Another Elegant Sight 76
[87] At the Time of the Gosechi Festival 77
[88] One Day Her Majesty Brought along a Bewa
    called Nameless 77
[89] I Remember an Occasion 77
[90] Infuriating Things 77
[91] Things it's Infuriating and Embarrassing to Witness 77
[92] Startling and Disconcerting Things 78
[93] Regrettable Things 78
[94] At the Time of the Abstinence and the Prayer of the
    Fifth Month 78
[95] It was while we were in the Office of the
    Empress's Household 78
[96] There Was a Large and Distinguished Gathering 79
[97] The Emperor Paid a Visit 79
[98] One Wet Day During the Endless Rains 79
[99] There Could Have Been no more Splendid
    Celebrations Conceivable 79
[100] A Branch of Plum from which the Blossoms had Fallen 79

Chapter Four: Things that Look Ordinary but Become
Extraordinary when Written 81
[101] Around the End of the Second Month 81
[102] Things that have Far to Go...81
[103] Masahiro is a Great Laughing-stock............................81
[104] Things that are Distressing to See...............................81
[105] Things that are Hard to Say..81
[106] Barrier Gates 82
[107] Forests 82
[108] Plains...82
[109] Around the End of the Fourth Month 82
[110] Common Things that Suddenly Sound Special.............83
[111] Things That Lose by Being Painted.............................83
[112] Things That Gain by Being Painted 84
[113] Winter is Best When it's Fearfully Cold......................84
[114] Moving Things 84
[115] It's Delightful to be on Retreat..................................85
[116] Deeply Irritating Things 86
[117] Miserable-looking Things 86
[118] Things that Look Stiflingly Hot 87
[119] Embarrassing Things 87
[120] Awkward and Pointless Things 87
[121] Prayers and Incantations 87
[122] Awkward and Embarrassing Things.............................87
[123] The Regent was to Emerge from the Black Door..........88
[124] It is Beautiful the Way the Water Drops Hang so Thick.88
[125] When we Gathered the Herbs......................................88
[126] In the Second Month an Event Called the Selection 88
[127] One Day someone Idly Said...88
[128] After the Late Regent's Death 89
[129] One Evening, Secretary Controller Yukinari 89
[130] One Dark Moonless Night...90

[131] The Year of Mourning......................................90
[132] Occasions When the Time Drags by 90
[133] Things that Relieve such Occasions 91
[134] Worthless Things...91
[135] Things that are Truly Splendid 91
[136] After the Regent had Departed this Life 92
[137] It's Towards the Middle of the First Month.................93
[138] A Good-looking Man 93
[139] It's Also Amusing to See 93
[140] Alarming-looking Things 93
[141] Things that Look Fresh and Pure 93
[142] Distasteful-looking Things.................................93
[143] Things that Make the Heart Lurch with Anxiety.............94
[144] Endearingly Lovely Things 94
[145] Times When Someone's Presence Produces
       Foolish Excitement..95
[146] Things with Terrifying Names 95
[147] Things that Look Ordinary but Become Extraordinary
       when Written..97
[148] Repulsive Things...98
[149] Occasions When Something Inconsequential
       has its Day...98
[150] People who Look as if Things are Difficult for Them 99

*Chapter Five: Things now Useless that recall a
Glorious Past* *101*
[151] People who Seem Envious 101
[152] Things Whose Outcome you Long to Know.....................101
[153] Occasions for Anxious Waiting..............................101
[154] When the Empress was in Mourning for the
       Previous Regent 102
[155] The Name Kokiden Referred to the High Consort 103
[156] Things now Useless that recall a Glorious Past...........103

[157] Situation you have a Feeling will Turn out Badly 103

[158] Sutra Reading.. 104

[159] Things that are Near Yet Far.. 104

[160] Things that are Far Yet Near.. 104

[161] Wells 105

[162] Plains... 105

[163] Court Nobles 107

[164] Nobles 107

[165] Acting Provisional Governors...................................... 107

[166] Commissioners.. 107

[167] Priests 107

[168] Ladies 107

[169] Sixth-rank Chamberlains 108

[170] A Place Where a Lady Lives Alone 108

[171] The Home of a Lady in Court Service.......................... 108

[172] One Day in the Ninth Month.. 108

[173] It is Quite Delightful When the Snow is Falling........... 108

[174] Once During the Reign of the Former
       Emperor Murakami... 110

[175] The Lady Known as Miare no Seji................................ 110

[176] When I First Went into Court Service........................... 111

[177] People who Feel Smug.. 111

[178] Nothing is More Splendid Than Rank.......................... 111

[179] Awe Inspiring Things.. 112

[180] Illnesses.. 112

[181] It is Delightful to See One Who is a Great Ladies' Man112

[182] It's the Middle of a Fiercely Hot Day 112

[183] The Floorboards of the Southern or Perhaps the
       Eastern Aisle... 113

[184] It is Enchanting to Overhear 113

[185] Things That Prove Disillusioning 113

[186] It's Very Unseemly For a Man...................................... 113

[187] Winds 113

[188] The Day after a Typhoon.................................. 113
[189] Elegantly Intriguing Things 114
[190] Islands 114
[191] Beaches 114
[192] Bays.. 114
[193] Woods... 116
[194] Temples 116
[195] Sutras.. 116
[196] Buddhas 117
[197] Chinese Writings 117
[198] Tales 118
[199] Darani Incantations 119
[200] Musical Performances.................................... 119

Chapter Six: Things That No one Notices *121*
[201] Games 121
[202] Dances.. 122
[203] Plucked Instruments...................................... 122
[204] Wind Instruments 123
[205] Spectacles... 123
[206] Around the Fifth Month................................. 124
[207] When it's Fearfully Hot................................. 124
[208] On the Evening of the Fourth Day of the Fifth Month. 124
[209] On the Way to the Kamo Shrine 124
[210] At the End of the Eighth Month 124
[211] Soon After the End of the Eight Month 124
[212] Setting off to Climb the Slope 124
[213] The Sweet Flag Leaves From the Fifth Month.... 125
[214] A Well-scented Robe 125
[215] On a Bright Moonlit Night 125
[216] Things That Should be Big 125
[217] Things That Should be Small.......................... 126
[218] Things a House Should Have 127

[219] On Your Way Somewhere 127
[220] It Irritates me More Than Anything 127
[221] I Heard People Saying There'd been a Man in the
Long Room who had no Business Being There 127
[222] When Her Majesty Was in the Sanjo Palace 128
[223] When the Nurse Taifu Went off to Hyoga 128
[224] Once When I was in Retreat at Kiyomizu Temple 128
[225] Posting Stations 128
[226] Shrines 128
[227] The Ichijo Palace Went by the Name of 'The
Temporary Palace, ... 129
[228] Among the People Who Show You 129
[229] It's Lovely to See a Day When the Snow Lies Thick 129
[230] It is Also Charming to Witness 130
[231] Hills 131
[232] Things That Fall 131
[233] Kinds of Sun 131
[234] Kinds of Moon 131
[235] Stars 131
[236] Clouds 132
[237] Things That Create a Disturbance 137
[238] Slovenly Looking Things 137
[239] People of Rough Speech 137
[240] People Who Are Smug and Cocky 138
[241] Things That Just Keep Passing By 138
[242] Things That No One Notices 138
[243] I Particularly Despise People Who Express
Themselves Poorly in Writing 139
[244] Horrid Filthy Things 140
[245] Terrifying Things 140
[246] Things That Give You Confidence 140
[247] A Son-in-law is Brought In 140
[248] Being Disliked by Others 140

[249] Men Have Most Unlikely and Peculiar Feelings 140
[250] Nothing is More Wonderful Than Sympathy................ 140

Chapter Seven: Things of Splendour and Spectacle *141*
[251] I Really Cannot Understand People Who Get Angry.... 141
[252] The Thing about Someone's Face................................. 142
[253] Old-fashioned People Put on Their Gathered Trousers 142
[254] Once Towards the Middle of the Tenth Month............. 142
[255] Captain Narinobu Was Wonderful at Distinguishing
       People's Voices.. 143
[256] No One had Sharper Ears than the Minister of the
       Treasury 143
[257] Things That Give You Pleasure 143
[258] I Was Talking With Some People in Her Majesty's
       Presence 144
[259] On the Twenty-First Day of the Second Month 144
[260] Venerable Things 146
[261] Songs... 146
[262] Gathered Trousers 148
[263] Hunting Costumes 149
[264] Shifts... 149
[265] Formal Train Robes... 150
[266] Fan Ribs 150
[267] Cypress Fans 150
[268] Deities 151
[269] Promontories... 151
[270] Huts... 151
[271] The Calling of the Night Watch is a Wonderful Thing.. 152
[272] At Noon on a Beautiful Sunny Day............................ 152
[273] Captain Narinobu... 152
[274] You Have a Lover Who Always Sends You a Next
       Morning Poem.. 152
[275] Things of Splendour and Spectacle............................ 153

[276] When There are Great Thunderclaps 153

[277] The Kongenroku Screen is a Fascinating Thing 153

[278] A Seasonal Directional Taboo 154

[279] The Snow was Piled High 155

[280] The Little Boy Employed by the Yin-Yang
      Masters is Terribly Clever 155

[281] In the Third Month, I Left the Court 155

[282] On the Twenty-Fourth Day of the Twelfth Month 155

[283] When Gentlewomen in the Palace Leave 155

[284] Things That Imitate 158

[285] Things One Must be Wary Of 158

[286] A Certain Officer of the Right Gate Watch 158

[287] The Mother of the Ohara Gentleman 158

[288] The Letter Narihira's Mother the Princess Sent Him 158

[289] It's Terribly Depressing to Discover 158

[290] If a Mere Common Woman 159

[291] The Officers of the Left and Right Gate Watch 159

[292] Grand Counsellor Korechika Presented
      Himself One Day 159

[293] I Was Sitting One Day with Bishop Ryuen's
      Nurse Mama 159

[294] There was a Man Whose Mother Dies 159

[295] A Certain Gentlewoman was Courted by the
      Governor of Totomi's Son 160

[296] Stealing and Illicit Conversation with Someone 160

[297] Can it be True? 160

ι

Introduction to Common Things That Are Suddenly Special by Brenda Liddy

Who Was Sei Shōnagon?

Sei Shōnagon (966-1017) was a Japanese author who served as a court lady to the Empress Teishi in the mid-Heian period around the year 1,000. During her period at the imperial court, she composed her 'pillow book' which was in effect a collection of observations, impressions, opinions on everyday life in the court, including the highs and lows of aristocratic life. You might say Sei with her witty and sometimes pithy, sometimes unflattering remarks was a forerunner of the Tweetosphere...a kind of early modern tweeter!

What is The Pillow Book (枕草子 makura no sōshi?)

My discovery of her book was a random incident that I am sure Sei would have endorsed. On one of my trips abroad a Chinese doctor on the flight recommended Sei's *Pillow Book*. I am an early modern researcher on women's writing in the renaissance period so of course my interest was piqued. After reading her book, I became an avid fan and was surprised to learn that she had a vibrant online presence in terms of academic papers, blogs and translations. This style of writing is known as zuihitsu which is basically a random collection of thoughts, and reflections. The kangi words mean follow the brush. As I was admiring the cherry blossoms in Kamakura during my visit to Japan in 2005, I was amazed that my Zen world of meditation and koan study were converging with my writing world where Sei Shōnagon's Pillow Book had taken centre stage in my reading and research.

Why Did I Decide to Base my Inspirational Memoir on Sei Shōnagon's Book?

It just grew out of a sense of connection with the style. I have written two academic books on women's drama, which are aimed at a scholarly readership. Since I have embarked on teaching creative writing in university and community settings, I am often asked for examples of my own writing. So the need to address this gap, as well as a deeper wish to connect with the East spurred me on to get going. The style suited my lifestyle as most of my time is taken up with my teaching career and also developing my meditation practice. Also when I became a lay ordained practitioner in the Soto Zen lineage, my teacher Paul Haller gave me a Japanese name, Kai Getsu Yūdo, Ocean Moon Fearless Way.

CHAPTER ONE:

Things That Induce Half-Heartedness

[1] *The Seasons*

In spring crocuses bloom in the garden. Daffodils appear. Snow melts and the lambs are born. March hares box. It's Lent and I make sacrifices. I go to confession and communion. It's time to wear my Easter bonnet. Children eat Easter eggs.

I think that Matsuo Basho, 1644-1694, a famous Japanese poet of the Edo period conveys the spirit of spring in this haiku:

On a journey
Resting beneath the cherry blossoms.
I feel myself to be in a Noh play.

This cherry tree is near my home in Kansas Avenue

In summer, I enjoy the warm weather. I have a holiday. The Orangemen march on the Twelfth of July. I recall summers in Swatragh where I grew up on a farm. The cows flicked the flies off with their long tails.

In autumn, the leaves turn red and yellow. I like this season. It is a comfort to the poets. I like to see the leaves dancing on the trees, some of them holding on to the bitter end. I remember eating nuts and apples in the country and gathering plums. Then we played Halloween games, but not trick or treat and not dressing up. Now everyone wants to dress up. The University of Ulster students on the train journey from Belfast to Coleraine were talking about dressing up as pirates and cat women. One girl said she wore the bottoms of her silk pyjamas last year and that they were baggy. Students outside Queen's were talking about buying corsets and going as swans. Not a mention of Frankenstein or Dracula but I am sure there will be a surfeit of monsters in the city, come the 31st.

This bridge is outside Toome.

In the winter my house in Kansas Avenue is freezing cold and I dread the snow as I have to drive to my work. Last year my window washer stopped working and I had to pull in at a garage to clean my windscreen. It was frightening. I was trying to get to Coleraine to teach a class at 9am and my university inspector was coming out to observe the lesson. It was the 6th December 2010. I will never forget that date. It was as if the elements conspired against me to stop me getting to my destination.

[2] *My Favourite Months*
I like March, August and September but as Sei Shōnagon says, there is something beautiful about every month.

[3] *I Love the New Year*
I like the New Year. Since the 1998 Good Friday Agreement, Belfast City Council has organised an open air concert. However it was cancelled this year and the council said the reason for this were rising costs and falling numbers. It is said that young people want to go clubbing and older people prefer to stay in. However for some strange reason I listened to a radio programme about a midnight fireworks display along the Embarcadero, near Pier 14.

Sei Shōnagon served in the Empress Teishi's court during the Heian period (794–1185). In this entry she describes the festival of the full-moon gruel where a bowl of gruel is given to the emperor. The rest of the day seemed to consist of the women chasing each other with gruel sticks and the atmosphere in the palace was light-hearted. Maybe April's Fool Day meets Halloween 'trick or treat'.

Shōnagon recalls going to the palace to see a procession of blue horses. Recently, I watched the horses parading around before the start of the Qatar Prix de L'Arc de Triomphe, on October 1st 2011. I do not usually watch sport but I was intrigued by the very interesting commentary by Clare Balding. You rarely see female sports commentators. She moved around the paddocks, pointing out the owners in white suits, and expensive dresses and the jockeys.

There was a string of fillies including the four year-old Sarafina, trained by Alain De Royer-Dupre at 5/1 and Ed Dunlop's Snow Fairy at 10/1. Viewers all around the world watched this mile and a half race. Also there were two Japanese horses, Hiruno D'amour ridden by Shinji Fujita and Nakayama Festa, ridden by Masayoshi Ebina. These are horses with chances. I did some research on Nakayama Festa and found out that she was foaled on 5th April 2006. Her sire was Stay Gold, her grandsire Sunday Silence, and her dam was Dear Wink and her damsire, Tight Spot. "We had planned to work at a different ground," trainer Yoshitaka Ninomiya explained, "but we had to resort back to the usual track when his temper got the better of us. Still, his movement was good and he looked fine. He's ready to race." I also found out that Mitsugu Kon, Hiruno D'amour's trainer said that the filly's sweating was 'different from last week' and that 'his breathing is good.' [1]

Danedream ridden by Andrasch Starke won the race. Here she is spread-eagling to the finishing line. Sarafina could not get into to it.

I also watched Haydock's 3.05 race and the commentator said things like "This horse has a place in people's hearts" and "the roof has come off the stadium." I like listening to the commentary. And the horses have some great names, such as Kauto Star and Weird Owl. 'L'Extraterrestre' translates to 'The Extraterrestrial'. On Saturday 19th November, Kauto Star made it four victories in the Betfair Chase. He won the race in 2006, 2007 and 2009. He beat Long Run by eight lengths. I also watched the Ascot 3.20 and the commentator said, "there was no hiding place out there today." He referred to a horse called 'I'm Singing the Blues'.

She also described poor candidates who come to the palace and present their petitions and how the ladies-in-waiting made fun of them when they had gone.

In Ireland the New Year is a time to make New Year Resolutions, join a gym, start a diet, and then break them before the end of the month, if not the week.

[4] *On the Third Day of the Third Month*

March is one of my favourite months, as I stated earlier. There is probably no greater sight than golden daffodils coming into bloom. I love driving out to Newtownabbey as there are rows of them planted along the dual carriageway. Their golden heads dance in the wind. St Patrick's Day, the 17th March is a great day for celebrating our national saint. Since the Good Friday Agreement in 1998, there have been more public celebrations in Belfast.

I took this photograph on 17th March 2011 and as you can see two young women sport tall green hats and there is probably a link to St Patrick but again it looks as if commercialism wins out every time. I also saw young men with green glitter newsboy hats and red curly beards, and women wearing green tinsel wigs, long 80s style neon fishnet gloves and trailing green and white turkey feather boas round their necks. Some kids brandished giant inflatable hammers and mallets, and sported lime green converse shoes. Some women wore green tutus, cowboy hats and wristbands festooned with St Patrick's Day green. There were 'kiss me I'm Irish' on tee-shirts and some carried cans of Carling beer. It had a certain *Mardi Gras* feel to it and I suppose there is no harm in greening up once a year.

[5] *Spring Blossoms*

I took this picture in the spring as I was walking down the Antrim Road. These cherry trees are in the grounds of the

Antiochian Orthodox Church of St Ignatius, which was formerly St James', Church of Ireland. It is situated at the corner of Antrim Road and Cliftonville Road.

I like it best in the spring and when the blossoms start to fall, they make a soft pink carpet underneath your feet, like soft pink popcorn. I have never been in this church and know nothing about their faith. After looking at their website today, I have ascertained that it is close to my own Catholic faith. I do not see many differences in that they accept the Holy Trinity, the Creed, the sacraments and Mary as the mother of God.

[6] *Every Day is a Good Day*

Staying on the subject of religion, and spring, I attended a Zen retreat in Benburb this year. Paul Haller, abbot of San

Francisco Zen Centre, led the Sesshin. One of the koans in Zen is "every day is a good day." Although I am a practising Catholic, I have a Zen practice as well.

This is a picture of me in the grounds of Benburb Priory after a Zen Retreat. Ummon said to his disciples, "I do not ask you to  say anything about before the fifteenth day of the month, but say something about after the fifteenth day of the month."[3] Because no monk could reply, Ummon answered himself and said, "Every day is a good day!" Ummon, (862–949) was a famous Chinese Zen master in the Tang dynasty period. He was famous for his one liners such as 'guan' which means 'barrier'. An unconventional teacher, he used to chase away people who tried to write down his teachings, and with a blow of his staff he would accuse them of one day trying to sell them. Very prophetic. What I understand from his koan, 'every day is a good day' is that we have to endeavor to let go of the past and not focus on the future. The only reason we do not rejoice in the present is because we are carrying bitter memories and harbouring anxious forebodings about the future. As I write this today I am anxious about the repairs I have to carry out in my home and where I will get the money. Also I bought £330 of heating oil from Knockbracken Fuels this afternoon and it's a lot of money to find before payday. But good things happened to me today as well. I attended a film journalism course and we discussed Andrea Arnold's new adaptation of *Wuthering Heights*. Carol Murphy, the tutor, taught us the difference between dramatic and epic films. For example, *In the Name of the Father* is dramatic and *Bronson* is epic. In dramatic style, the mechanics are kept hidden from the audience. As for causality, there is a chain of interrelated actions; characters change in the course of the action and by the end there is closure, brought about by the character's actions. In the epic, there is a narrative voice, which shapes our understanding of the film. Cause and effect are more open ended, and the character may not necessarily change in the film. The ending is not conclusive and there is space for audience participation.

[7] *Different Ways of Speaking*

Some people in Belfast speak 'broad Belfast' or with a 'Norn Iron' accent. To say hello, you would say "bout ye,' and you might add 'mucker,' meaning friend. I overhead a man saying to a woman who had ventured out on a windy day, 'You're fond, coming out a day like that.' Sometimes people will use the expression, 'Come here, 'till I tell ye, or 'you're havin me on' or 'I'm just out for a wee dander,' or 'I didn't come down the Lagan in a bubble.' 'Aye' means yes, 'scundered' means embarrassed, 'foundered' means cold, and 'bake' means face. All Belfast people love fried bread and 'taty' bread made from potatoes is very popular. 'Taty bread' is also rhyming slang for dead.

At the moment I am working a few mornings in Ballymena and as I had some free time, I walked into the town centre. I heard what I believe to be strong Ulster Scots accents. For example a woman in the Vision charity shop said, "He's oot," meaning he's out, and 'mere' for 'more'. Then in a cafe called the Bayleaf, I had the feeling I was in 'Disney Land.' People said he 'disney' want this, and he 'canny' do and he was 'no' there, for not there. I heard someone say that Elizabethan English is still spoken in this area. But there is an immediacy about it and I honestly say that I like this accent.

Today on the 'Talk Back' show on Radio Ulster, the topic was homelessness. A taxi driver phoned in and he had a Belfast accent. He said, "You know what I mean like," and peppered his phrases with the word "absolutely."

[8] *Elegant Things*

Elegant things I can think of are swans. I live beside the Waterworks, and there are beautiful swans there.

I often walk around the park and marvel at their beauty and elegance. I like to see the cygnets swimming behind their parents. They say swans are monogamous. Sometimes you can hear them hissing and this can seem out of character.

One of my favourite fairy stories is 'The Ugly Duckling,' by Hans Christian Anderson. When you see the mottled brown of the young swan's wings changing to white, you cannot help but think how amazing the transformation is. Bruno Bettelheim said that the Ugly Duckling is not really a hero as he does not undergo any major trial. I was teaching Christopher Vogler's *The Writer's Journey* in Queen's last semester and I presented the class with the hero journey's model. Going from the ordinary world to the special world, the hero is called to an adventure, he meets his mentor, comes up against enemies and when he crosses the

threshold, he enters the innermost cave, wins the prize and brings the gift back to the community. Technically the Ugly Duckling remains in the farmyard with the pedestrian ducks until he grows into an enormous and elegant swan and flies away. His destiny unfolds rather than him taking affirmative action.

Another story which impresses me about swans is 'The Children of Lir.' I taught this story in the Northern Regional College last year. It was taken from a book called *Irish Tales and Sagas* by Ulick O'Connor and illustrated by Pauline Bewick. The story is about the wicked stepmother, Aoife who arranges an enchantment where her stepchildren Fionnuala, Aodh, Fiachra and Conn, are turned into swans. They spend 300 years on Lough Derravaragh and 300 years in the Sea of Moyle and 300 years on the waters of the Atlantic by Erris and Inishglory. Thomas Moore's song 'Silent O Moyle, Be the Roar of Thy Water' tells the story of the Children of Lir.

[9] *The Cat who lived in the Palace*

This anecdote gives an insight into the Heian court's preoccupations, which may seem petty to a modern reader. We hear how a precious cat, beloved of Her Majesty, has been 'awarded the headdress of nobility' and given the name Lady Myōbu which was given to ladies of the fifth rank in the imperial palace. There was also a fox deity named Myōbu. In my Zen studies, I have been reading a book on the fox koan and folklore, called *Shifting Shape, Shaping Text. Philosophy and Folklore in the Fox Koan*, by Steven Heine.

Although Northern Ireland where I live is part of the United Kingdom, and technically Queen Elizabeth II is the Queen, I have never actually seen any royalty in the flesh, never mind an empress. However after reading this excerpt, regarding the misadventure of the palm-leaf carriages not being able to enter through the east gate of Narimasa's courtyard, which meant the ladies-in-waiting were somewhat discomfited, having to walk a small distance from the gate to the house, the main problem seemed to have been one of personal vanity and I found this amusing. I would not call myself a royalist but I do enjoy reading about a world with all its customs and mannerisms that seem somewhat outdated. But by the same measure, women are obsessed about their looks, weight and so forth. In a recent film, *The Devil Wears Prada* one of the characters says that "She doesn't deserve it, she eats carbs for Chrissake." This statement has lingered in my head. Last year I marked examination papers and one of the essays was about body image. So many of these sixteen years-olds had an unhealthy preoccupation with their body image but at the same time some were aware of the media tricks of air brushing. I had never heard of Gok Wan before but I was amazed to see what an impression he had made on some of the students. He apparently gives women confidence, no matter what their size or shape. One student commented that 'he must really love her because he met up with her and she was not even wearing makeup'. If that is the prevailing attitude among young girls, I am seriously concerned. I went to Loreto Convent in the mid-sixties and I would never have dreamed of wearing makeup. Now I see they are applying oodles of the stuff in the toilets of the train station in Coleraine. Similarly the young students in the college in which I teach are often preening themselves in the ladies' toilets. I suppose young people have the opportunity to participate in the fashion industry but education gives them the chance to be critical. However I do not think we should underestimate the tremendous pressure that young people are put under to look good, dress well, listen to the right music and so forth.

As I am writing this the whole debacle of ruptured breast implants has been in the news. I have been listening in horror to the testimonies of these poor women who are been left in an awful predicament. I was really struck by one woman who said re PIP implants, "My breasts are stuffed with the same substance which is in this mattress. I looked up the acronym and it stands for 'Poly Implant Prothese.' The bottom line, I feel is that women's health has been put in jeopardy because of these implants. Some people are of the opinion that nobody forced the women to have the breast enhancements but surely there must be an underlying perception that big breast equals sexiness and bee sting size breasts equals frigidity. I blame the media! One woman I read about says she was size 32 and she did not feel attractive enough so that's why she opted for the implants. Would men stuff their chests with implants? I doubt it! My pillow book is definitely not stuffed with PIP filling. However I would like to congratulate the Health Secretary, Andrew Lansley who has hit out at the private care providers, and is not letting them off the hook. If they fail to live up to their moral duty by offering free scans etc. the NHS will cover the costs.

Maybe I am just a middle aged Victorian but I thought doctors and surgeons swore a Hippocratic Oath or something like that, vowing they would protect and save life. I read somewhere that doctors are called doctors because they used to be academic doctors like moi. The root of the word is the Latin, 'doceo,' 'I teach'... in medieval Europe the term *licentia docendi* meant a licence to teach.

But I do not want to get on my soapbox, so I will return to matters royal. So returning to the imperial themes, I found this in Bagehot's blog which made me think of *The Pillow Book:*

> On May 25th the monarch delivered the Queen's Speech, amid the traditional pageantry of crowns and coaches, cavalrymen in dazzling cuirasses, Black Rod, trumpeters and Ken Clarke, the justice secretary and Lord Chancellor, wearing an absurd wig.[4]

Yes we may not have an empress but we still retain ceremony, crowns, coaches, cavalrymen in cuirasses, and the Lord Chancellor in a ridiculous wig.

I would like to quote the next section, which shows that beneath all the pomp and ceremonial spectacle, two men in grey pinstripe suit give grim forecast from the foyer of the Treasury:

> The previous day, two nondescript men had given a dry press conference in the atrium of the Treasury, at which they discussed the government's consultancy bill and tax budget.

As for the manoeuvrings involved in the Queen and her entourage moving I can assure you it is not as simple as moving diagonally on a chess board. The Royal Family's home away from home would obviously have to be a castle and I have heard the name Balmoral mentioned quite often. I have read that she and the family go there from August to October.

Note to Reader

I just want to point out that the translation on which I have based my book was translated by Ivan Morris. It's an excellent book. Regrettably I incurred a fine at the University of Ulster from where I had borrowed Morris's book. I am so busy driving to the various campuses in the Northern Regional College that I forgot to renew it as well as a bunch of other books belonging to other libraries. So I bought my own from Amazon Books. I never noticed that it was a different translation. I should have noticed this as I have just published an article on translation strategies. This is the abstract:

> When Katherine Philips produced her translation of *Pompey*, she was unaware that she set in motion a trend for classical translations in Irish theatre. As J.-P. Short stresses, her translation was 'the first real translation of the Restoration and it was put on for the first time in 1663 in the newly-opened Smock-Alley Theatre in Dublin'. This

article will examine Katherine Philips's translation strategies in her play *Pompey* and it will examine her choice of subject for the Restoration stage. *Pompey* (1663) was translated by Katherine Philips in the early years of the Restoration. Véronique Desnain observes that Philips was aware of the need to offer a play which commented on the aftermath of the war and the need to achieve political stability and the wish to establish a cultured Protestant Anglo-Irish identity. Philips used translation in a competent manner to mediate the transitional events of the newly restored monarchy. Translation, as Kay Gilliland Stevenson has pointed out, performs an important function in drama in this turbulent period. 'Translation is a phenomenon particularly interesting when considering self-consciousness about periods, or transitions.'

This translation by Meredith McKinney has a different running order, but I shall just start at excerpt 10.

[10] *Mountains*

Shōnagon mentions Ogura Mountain and Mount Kase. I looked up Ogura Mountain on the internet and I am delighted to find out that it is referred to as Poet's Mountain. *Ogura Hyakunin Isshui* is a famous Japanese anthology of poetry which consists of a hundred poems by a hundred poets, written mostly in the late Heian period. The poems known as 'waka' are five line poems of 31 syllables, 5, 7, 5, 7, 7. The mountain that I love best is the Cave Hill Mountain in north Belfast. Not only does it inspire poets, but it is said that its profile of a huge head inspired Jonathan Swift to write *Gulliver's Travels*.

[11] *Markets*

St George's Market in Belfast was built between 1890 and1896. It is one of the most famous markets in Ireland. You will find the following items at this market: spices, chutneys and chocolates, scented candles, clothes, jewellery, recycled goods, household goods, antiques, garden plants, health and beauty products and seaweed products.

Since The Good Friday Agreement 1998, we have a Continental Market at Christmas. It is located in the grounds of the City Hall. There are mouth-watering foods for example, olives, speciality cheeses, crepes, French tarts and not forgetting Spanish paella, and Bratwurst, a highly seasoned German sausage. I love to buy a hot chocolate and walk around the various stalls, drinking in the sights and smells. As a vegetarian, I am not attracted to the rare meats stalls, which include alligator, wild boar and kangaroo. There are also art and craft stalls and once I bought a beautiful turquoise ring. For the garden enthusiast there are a range of trees and shrubs and garden furniture.

A typical afternoon at the Continental Market, December 2011

In the market a sign that read Greek Specialities: All Pure Vegetarian. I had no idea when I took this shot that it was a vegetarian stall. Instant karma! I have been a vegetarian for twenty five years. The recent scandal in regard to horse meat entering the meat food chain has only strengthened this opinion.

[12] *Peaks*

Shōnagon seems to distinguish between mountains and peaks. The first peak she refers to, Yuzuruha mountain peak, is near Fukura, Hyōgo, Japan. Slieve Donard, which means *Sliabh Dónairt*, "Dónairt's mountain", is part of the Mourne Mountains and is the highest peak in Northern Ireland. From the summit on a clear day, you can see Belfast, thirty miles to the north and Dublin, fifty- five miles to the south. It is said the Mourne Mountains was the place where St Patrick banished the snakes from Ireland.

[13] *Plains*

Shōnagon refers to Mika Plain. I found this poem written by Chu-Nagon Kanesuke which contains a reference to Mika Plain:

Oh! rippling River Izumi,
That flows through Mika plain:[5]

The area around the river Shannon is referred to as the central plain of Ireland where the underlying rock is limestone with a coating of glacial drift. The Burren, an area of outstanding beauty in the Shannon region, also consists of limestone. The rolling hills of the Burren are composed of limestone pavements with criss-crossing cracks known as 'grikes', leaving isolated rocks called 'clints'. Oliver Cromwell famously described the Burren as: "Not enough wood to hang a man, not enough water to drown a man, and not enough soil to bury a man."

[14] *River Pools*

This entry is so refreshing to read, and it offers a moment of reflection. As Sei comments, 'I wonder what hidden depths someone saw in its heart, to give it such a name.' It seems as if she is making a list but as Matilda Leyser points out her lists are not mere inventory:

Even within Shonogan's simplest lists—lists of mountains, rivers, plants, birds – we are made aware that the items being listed are not simply natural forms but linguistic constructs. The act of naming, that primal moment when a word, a sound, attaches to a concept inside a mind, the moment when classification occurs, is dramatized.[6]

I also found this wonderful haiku which includes the name 'kashiko':

blooming plum—
the voices of children
sound reverent

ume saku ya kodomo no koe no ana kashiko[7]

[15] *Bodies of Water*

Shōnagon comments that 'Lake Biwa is so special'. Lake Biwa, the largest freshwater lake in Japan, is on the outskirts of Kyoto. I live near a body of water known as the Waterworks. It was bombed during World War II as the Germans thought it was a reservoir. Another body of water with which I am familiar is Lough Neagh. It is also a large freshwater lake. It is said that Finn McCool, a figure from Irish mythology, formed the lough by scooping out the soil and flinging it at a rival Scottish giant. He missed and it landed on the middle of the Irish sea, and became known as the Isle of Man. It is interesting that the Celts talk about loughs. The Scots refer to lochs, as in Loch Ness, where supposedly a monster resides. There is a famous lake in Sligo known as Lough Gill. W. B. Yeats wrote a famous poem about it:

I will arise and go now and go to Innisfree
And a small cabin build there, of clay and wattles made.

The poem the 'Lake Isle of Innisfree' 1888, was written to establish a distinct genre of Irish poetry. Loughs and lochs seem to inspire legends about monsters and giants, whereas lakes inspire nostalgia.

[16] *Imperial Tombs*

Imperial tombs are usually associated with the Ming and Qing dynasties. In Ireland we have dolmens or portal tombs which consist of two or three standing stones and a huge capstone. There is a famous dolmen in the Burren called Poulnabrone. It dates back to the Neolithic period and was probably used for ceremonies and rituals.

[17] *Ferry Crossings*

I have crossed over from Portaferry to Strangford many times, and I have fond memories of making this trip. Van Morrison wrote a song, 'Coney Island' which refers to Strangford:

Out all day birdwatching
And the craic was good
Stopped off at Strangford Lough
Early in the morning
Drove through Shrigley taking pictures
And on to Killyleagh.

[18] *Large Buildings*

Since 1998, we have many new buildings in Belfast, for example, The Victoria Centre, the Waterfront Hall and the Odyssey. I love them all, especially the Waterfront, as I have gone to some really good events there, including *End Game,* by Samuel Beckett and *Othello* by William Shakespeare. I saw it in the Waterfront in March and there were a few schools in attendance during the performance. I recall one school girl saying to the other, "the white woman was having an affair with the black man," and I smiled to myself. But I do think the young girl made a point, for what they were seeing on the stage was the portrait of an inter-racial marriage, which interestingly enough is something different on the northern Irish stage, where mixed marriages are more the order of the day in the context of sectarianism.

[19] *Residences*

One of my favourite historic houses is Mount Stewart on the shores of Strangford Lough. The gardens, which were lovingly designed by Lady Edith Londonderry (1879-1959), contain many exotic plants which can survive in the Ards Peninsula's mild micro-climate. There is a Spanish Garden, an Italian Garden, a Maori Garden and a Sunken Garden. Japanese, Australian and South American influences are also a feature of these amazing grounds.

[20] *The Sliding Panels*

This is a lengthy entry and gives an insight into the sophisticated nature of the court life in classical Japan. The empress charges her ladies-in-waiting to 'just jot down any ancient poem that comes to you on the spur of the moment'. This command reminds me of the exercises I have completed at creative writing classes...a sort of Middle Ages writing prompt. It is interesting that Her Majesty commented, 'I just wanted to discover what was in your hearts.' I think I could base a whole creative writing class on this concept alone. The last creative writing class which I attended was Shalom Writers' Group on 29/02/12. This is an established group which has published a few anthologies, including some of my work. The poems presented that day were excellent. The first was 'Eddie and Ann' written by Noreen Campbell. It was about a couple in their nineties, who despite the many vagaries of life are still together. The next was 'Song of the Sitakund Waterfall' written by Rozana Ahmad Huq. It was about the way the water cascaded in a vortex of musical notes. Robert Kirk presented a poem called 'The Penitent Magdalene' which was his response to Georges de La Tour's painting. Christine Leckey wrote a poem entitled 'My Mother's Shoes' which did not fit her, because of the 'genetic gift' of inheriting her father's large feet. Denis O'Sullivan wrote, 'Wedding Weather', about the resentful clouds which cast racing shadows. Michael Scott's poem 'Contact' was about a barefoot walk on his lawn on a September morning. Tom Honey wrote one called 'Teco-Teco' about how picturesque poetry can seem from a distance. Jonathan wrote 'The Parthenologist's Girlfriend' which contains the line, 'To hell with Nebraska's Law.' Certainly not very Heian dynasty! I proffered 'The Death of Donegal,' which was about the death of Maura's cat:

The Death of Donegal

Deirdre's cat was called Donegal
That's where he came from
a small Heathcliff, cowering
inside Her brother's coat,
black and diabolical.

But he was an
Edgar Linton, in the
front parlour,
lapping milk and
purring benevolently.

Every morning he came back
With savage cuts after
Some nightly hostility.

His mother was
a tigress, his father
a black Panther.

Deirdre said her father talked
More to that black devil
Than he did to her.
Damian said, 'there is as
Much chance of daddy
parting with Donegal as
a cat leaving a thrush half eaten.'
He died on the last Saturday
of February and left us in
this dark alone where we
cannot find him.

[21] *Women without Prospect*

This entry is quite scathing towards women, 'who lead dull earnest lives and rejoice in their petty little pseudo-pleasures.' I like the way Shōnagon uses every opportunity to declare that working in the palace is a golden opportunity to learn the ways of the world. I studied Restoration comedy where the follies and foibles of court life were portrayed. Congreve's *The Way of The World* depicts a world of adulterous affairs and marriages based on dowries. Gergana Ivanova's comments on this passage are illuminating:

> This passage confirms not only the unfavourable per-
> ception of female attendants but also Sei's awareness of it.
> In addition to their vulnerable position within the court,
> their instability increased with the decline of Teishi's sa-
> lon since the fate of attendants was contingent on the
> political influence of their patrons.[8]

The humour, as Ivanova points out, helps Sei to promote and justify her role as a court attendant. A modern woman in today's world would not see service as particularly empowering. At the same time there is still the 'glass ceiling' where many women are still doing the three Cs, caring, cooking and cleaning.

[22] *Dispiriting Things*

This entry is most amusing and covers everything from a howling dog, to a still-birth to a botched exorcism. She also includes an un-rewarded messenger, and finally the hot bath taken as part of New Year's Eve's purificatory abstinence. We can still identify with the yapping dog, but the botched exorcism and the purificatory bath does seem somewhat removed from the 21st century.

I am quite an optimistic person but I can become dispirited now and again. Needless to say I hated bomb scares, which occurred frequently during the 'Troubles'. I wrote a book called *The Drama of War in the Theatre of Anne Devlin, Marie Jones, and Christina Reid, Three Irish Playwrights*. This is an excerpt from the introduction:

> Civil unrest in Northern Ireland over three decades, from 1969 to 1999, gave rise to an outpouring of women's drama, much of it anti-war in sentiment or with war as a theme. Until then, as Tylee, Turner and Cardinal point out, war drama tended to deal with male experience at the battlefront while female-authored plays focused on "women's experience behind the lines, especially on the home front, and on groups opposing war".[9]

Dr Jordan of UCD, made this very kind recommendation:

> Oftentimes writers are too close to the circumstances and contexts of their material; they lack the critical insights and distance necessary to make the work available to others less aware or less engaged with the circumstances from which the plays under discussion emerged.

That is most definitely not the case with this book. Brenda Liddy writes with the awareness of someone who is both a careful witness and astute com-mentator. Her work is simultane-ously nuanced and locally aware, yet functions just as easily on a more universal level. This excep-tionally insightful, astute and creative book is a decisive move towards addressing many of the analytical imbalances in current scholarship.

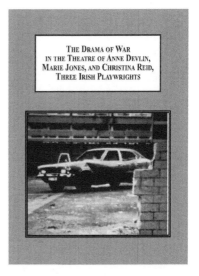

THE DRAMA OF WAR
IN THE THEATRE OF ANNE DEVLIN,
MARIE JONES, AND CHRISTINA REID,
THREE IRISH PLAYWRIGHTS

I think that is enough self-con-gratulation for now.

[23] *Occasional Things That Induce Half-Heartedness*
Sei seemed to find the religious ceremonies and fasting on-erous. I remember when I was young and out playing in the fields with my sister, my grandmother would call us in because it was Good Friday. I have a distinct memory of having to fast for three hours before the Good Friday ceremonies which start-ed at 3pm. It was usually cold and windy weather during Lent and we all went off sweets, which was huge sacrifice. I loved sweets especially Penny Chews, Rolo, Fruit Gums, and Love Hearts. I think it is funny when you see 'text me' on the modern Love Hearts. Recently I read an article by Mary Morrissy in the *Irish Times* on the topic of Good Friday. She wrote about the irony of a how religion and secular co-exist cheek by jowl in this beautiful city:

Despite the preponderance of glorious church archi-tecture, I think of Paris as a determinedly secular city. But every Good Friday, the Way of the Cross is re-enacted on the Rue Mouffetard in the heart of the Latin Quarter. Cobbled and narrow, the Rue Mouffetard winds its way gently up to Place du Panthéon. It was once the main route into Lutece, as Paris was called in Roman times. The Way of the Cross starts at the parish church of St Medard, at the bottom of the street.

I think it would be so wonderful to visit Paris and bear witness to this event. In my little church in Craigavole, where I attended Good Friday ceremonies, there were no spectacular enactments on cobbled street on Good Friday. Basically, the priest, Father Deery would have invited a reader on to the altar, to be narrator and the parishioners had to shout out 'crucify him, crucify him.' It was my first experience of theatre. It all seemed so hopeless but we did our best at that event to give Jesus a good send off. I think Pontius Pilate just went along with things and it was the way it had to be. The mob was quite contemptible. My mother's stepbrother, Terence Rafferty who later went on to qualify as a lawyer, had a great reading voice and he often performed the narrator's part. Then a huge cross was positioned at the centre of the altar, and we had to up one-by-one to kiss the wounded figure. I can remember all the fourteen stations vividly. Many times I made the Stations of the Cross, and my favourite one was the sixth where Veronica wiped the face of Jesus. I always felt so religious. The most foreboding station was the eighth where the women stand in a grief stricken clutch and Jesus gives them the chilling message, "Weep not for me, but for yourselves and your children."

It was all so beautiful back when the little pews were bulging with good country people, many of them my uncles, aunts and cousins, and the priest and the altar boys would process around the fourteen stations and we all genuflected in unison as the he uttered 'We adore thee O Christ and bless thee' and we would respond, 'Because by Thy Holy Cross, Thou hast redeemed the world.'

Then after some more prayers, the priest would recite the Stabat Mater prayer:

At the cross her station keeping
Stood the mournful Mother weeping
Close to Jesus to the last.

We would respond:

Holy Mother! Pierce me through
In my heart each wound renew
Of my Saviour crucified.

Like the heroine in *Rebecca* who dreamt she went back to Manderley, I go back to this little church where I learned Via Dolorosa, was baptised and made my First Holy Communion.

This year I attended the Good Friday ceremonies in Clonard Monastery. I was amazed to find out that an enactment was taking place after the service. The peace march began at 5pm outside Clonard Monastery on 6th April, 2012. After marching down Falls Road, the procession went to Northumberland Street and then to the Shankill Road. After leaving Shankill Road, the crowd headed to Springfield Road, where a small pedestrian gate was opened in the wall.

[24] *Things That People Despise*

The mention of the 'crumbling earth wall is timely, for at the moment I need my front wall mended. We got repairs done this spring to the tune of £15,000. It was a nightmare. Frank, my husband and Paul Haller, my Zen teacher wrote this poem jointly:

Kansas Undone
Belongings emptied
Familiarity undone
No going backwards

Rafters and bare brick
House, home totally exposed
Light floods through windows

I wrote this. One day after the builders had left, I noticed a yellow mixing bucket. It reminded me of the witches' cauldron in *Macbeth:*

You think they are in renovating.
You saw the PVC windows arriving.
But all they were doing was standing
Round the mixer bowl chanting:

Builder 1: Gather round the mixer bowl
Builder 2: Pour in water free of oils
Builder 3: Free of alkalis, and of sulphates
Builder 1: Mix in cement of
Limestone, iron, calcium
Silicon and aluminium
Builder 2: Make sure it is free
Of organic matter
Builder 3: Mix in sand
Builder 1: Sand, scorched by the sun
For days and night until it's ready
Builder 2: Stir and stir until it's smooth
Builder 3: Builders, builders
Sand and gravel, builder
Builder, let's make trouble
Builders, builders, spirit

Level, builders, builders
Shovel and trowel.

'Tis time, 'Tis time

[25] *Infuriating Things*

Sei describes many minor irritants which I can relate to. I think everyone hates long-winded pompous people. She men-
tions her annoyance at people warming their hands at a brazier. Poor Sei, so intolerant! I took this picture a few months ago during the Occupy Belfast protest which took place outside St Anne's Cathedral, Donegall Street. A few times I called into the camp and brought the protestors some re-freshments. One of the protestors was called Sadie, an American woman. She said she was left of the left movement. One night she came to the Zen Centre. I was very impressed by her. On one of the

occasions on which I called into the camp, a poor man was rest-ing in their camp and warming himself at the brazier. I was so impressed that the Occupy protestors were reaching out to the homeless. I loved seeing the camp every morning. It made me realise how attached I was to bricks and mortar. When I sat with the group I was aware of the strong fumes coming from the bra-zier. I could not tolerate it for very long. I did not want my clothes to smell of smoke.

She also describes an unsuccessful exorcism where the ex-orcist, much to everyone's annoyance cannot get the spirit to budge. Hollywood made a movie called *The Exorcist*. I have not personally met anyone who has had an exorcism but I have read that some Catholic priests still perform exorcisms. I found this course which is currently run by the Sacerdos Institute: VII Course on Exorcism and Prayers of Liberation - Rome, Italy - April 16–21, 2012. Its purpose is to train priests in the ministry of exorcism. Dominic Walker, the Bishop of Monmouth conducts exorcisms.

CHAPTER TWO:

Things to Make the Heart Go Faster

[26] *Things to Make the Heart Go Faster*
Sei says the sparrow with nestlings is one of the things that makes her heart go faster. This is a wonderfully poetic image. She also talks about the way dress-ing up makes her feel good.

This is an image of me play-ing Lady Catherine de Burgh in the Crescent Art Centre (August 2012)

I can identify with this. I had more sisters than Elizabeth Bennett, and remember when I started going to dances, with them, (Jane Austen's social mores did not prevail in the sixties and you did not have to wait on your older sisters to get married before you could go into society, or in Austenesque speak come 'out')... there would be a clutch of us around the mirror applying make-up liberally and putting on and then discarding a range of outfits. We had no transport and we had to beg for a lift. The dance hall we went to was called the Marian Hall, which was in Kilrea. It was the era of the big showbands and I recall jiving and waltzing every Friday night. There was no drink sold at the dances in those days and we as good Catholic girls were very virtuous. Much to my grandmother's chagrin, we wore miniskirts, maxi-skirts and trousers. She was a ninety year-old woman, a real stoic who reared us after the untimely death of our good mother. I begged my grandmother for £5 to buy a pair of Mary Quant boots. I was so happy, prancing about in them. Of course, they were quite impractical as I had to walk over a mile to the bus stop in order to get my bus for school and I soon had to abandon the boots. I remember when my sister Kate took a summer job in London, and when she returned she was wearing a cheese cloth maxi skirt and top...I could not believe there was this whole other world that was so full of beautiful fashionable clothes and that Kate was bringing the swinging sixties to our little farm house in the town land of Crossland. To be honest I can remember the sixties, which as the saying goes means that I was not there. As we headed towards the 'Troubles' things started to deconstruct. The education that I so craved was proving to be an emotional drain on me. Somehow the teachers did not realise that not all homes had an endless supply of money and when the Domestic Science teacher sent home a list of ingredients for a Christmas cake that each of her pupils were going to bake, Granny went ballistic. She read out the list as if incredulous: seven ounces of butter, four eggs, ¼ teaspoon of vanilla essence, two pounds of dried fruit, ¼ pound of chopped peel, half a pound of glace cherries, almonds, brandy and brown sugar. Then she added and that's not all, she wants you to bring in marzipan, royal icing, icing sugar and lemon juice. She said, 'just you tell the teacher that your granny is going to bake the cake herself.'

As for the 'Troubles' I remember going to Civil Rights marches. I was seeing these images of violence on the TV... and Radio Ulster was dominated by programmes about the political unrest. I will never forget how much security there was in the shops... your handbag was searched, and when if you were in Belfast, you were frisked going through the security gates. T.S. Eliot said London was an 'unreal city'. Belfast was a surreal city! After I finished my PhD, I wrote a book on the theatre of war.

I will never forget the day I got on a bus and headed off to Magilligan beach for an anti-internment protest. I can recall

John Hume's cream trench coat leading the march and suddenly the army firing plastic bullets and CS gas. It was scary. That was my first experience of being shot at by the British Army. The big rubber bullets went flying past us as we retreated. They were oblong in shape. I am so glad I was not hit by one of them. Those bullets made my heart go faster and my legs too. All I remember is racing back across the sand dunes and big black missile shaped bullets whizzing past my ankles. I found out later that the Parachute Regiment was there that day. The date was the 22nd January 1972. Eight days later, these 'Paras' would gun down 13 innocent people in Derry. In 1972 I had no idea what was happening. As Anne Devlin pointed out, 'there was all this big drama happening on the streets in Northern Ireland and we were all in rooms.'

[27] *Things That Make You Feel Nostalgic*

When I was a performer in the Land of Giants show, June 2012, one of the professional actors, Brigid gave us a great warm-up exercise to do first thing in the morning. She talked about finding your 'happy place.' I thought of the song from *The Sound of Music,* 'These are a few of my favourite things...when the dog bites, when the bee stings, when I am feeling low, I simply remember my favourite things, and then I don't feel so bad.' I went to the rehearsals, thinking that Land of Giants was something to do with Sinéad Morrissey's poetry. There was a scene where we all carried letters across the stage, with drummers on each side, fireworks, aerialists, actors waving flags in cherry pickers... unbelievable. What an extravaganza. The only thing was I felt a bit shell shocked as the rehearsals were physically demanding, and I thought I had fallen into a boot camp in hell...the rain was pouring through the roof, pigeons were looking down from the rafters in a menacing way and I was there training from 9am to 6pm for two entire weeks. Somehow I felt my body was not getting the routines. But on the positive side, the directors were so amazing and talented and after a few days I began to figure out what the show was about. Basically it was about showcasing Ireland as a land of giants: the line-up included the linen industry, ship building, Finn McCool, the Giant's Causeway, and not forgetting Swift's Gulliver, from *Gulliver's Travels*. Another moment of nostalgia occurred, if nostalgia can occur, was when James, our wonderful trainer, taught us this song at one of his warm-up exercises:

> I love the mountains.
> I love the rolling hills.
> I love the flowers.
> I love the daffodils.
> I love the fireside.
> When all the lights are low.

This brought tears to my eyes because the last time I sang this song was on the way back from a friend's house in Wicklow. It was one of the best holidays of my life.

The director sent us this wonderful message:

> In the face of all kinds of pressures - wind, rain, tiredness, a grumpy director, you were all simply wonderful! I know I said to some of you that if we all did well together, the audience wouldn't be able to tell who had been performing for twenty years and who had been rehearsing for two days.

Another thing that makes me nostalgic is dolls. I saw this book in the college: Making *Dolls and Dolls' Clothes* by Lia van Steenderen. Imagine, a book on how to make dolls' clothes.

This is a photograph from the cover page. I used to make dolls' clothes when I was young. Our house of six daughters was a cross between *Little Women* and the Brontes with a little bit of '*Little House on the Prairie.* I remember my cousin saying to me one day when he called in as I was busy sitting making dolls clothes: 'You're not surely still making dolls' clothes!' That did not dissuade me as I was at the very time he called experimenting with converting newspaper into a stiff petticoat for one on my creations. Alexander McQueen could not have been any more dedicated. I always like to read about famous talented designers. Apparently his garden was like the aftermath of a Glastonbury festival with dust of plaster of Paris in the air, red dye and silicone everywhere as he  worked on some new collection. That's the way I worked; pieces of silk and net and bits of velvet as I created on my latest design. I was speaking to my older sisters last week and they were telling me that when they were young my mother gave one of them a black doll. And that was in the fifties. They were also saying that sometimes they dressed up hot water bottles as dolls. Wasn't that wonderful!

To conclude this trip down memory lane, I will offer my poem on Barbie:

Barbie at Fifty: March 2009

I first appeared in 1959 at a New York Fair,
wearing a black and white bathing suit, made with care
and in my killer heels I walked with grace,
proud of my 40DD bust and slinky hips and skinny waist.

My creator, Ruth Handler, co-founder of Martel,
fashioned me from her own mind and a hint of Lilli.

I had what is now termed as a portfolio career,
model,
astronaut,
gymnast,
palaeontologist,
diplomat,
presidential candidate,
and not forgetting my stint as rapper.

Burberry, Versace, Armani,
designed clothes for me,
I was not just a clothes horse;
I had a strategy.

Unlike Cabbage Patch or Crolly Dolls,
I had élan, a Jackie O' style,
a pillbox hat and a fawn-coloured coat,
a metallic ball gown,
a sexy swimsuit and a suntan.

Although my proportions are anatomically incongruent,
And I spend too much time on my appearance,
I never dropped out in the sixties,
Or played truant,
took drugs,
or protested
on Capitol Hill.

I have remained a Virgin for fifty years,
and in my own way have adapted to all the sea-changes,
without losing my integrity.

I have welcomed my extended family of
cousins and siblings and all the

accessories,
But most of all I like
my pink Rolls-Royce.

And now I'm fifty,
I'm more robust than ever.
I have survived
The feminist backlash!
I am looking forward to
My new incarnations.
I am willing to take on new challenges;
I have considered,
a chat show host,
a famous jockey,
a brain surgeon,
a nuclear physicist,
a consultant psychiatrist,
a circus performer,
a surfer.

And who knows I might
even become an urban planner,
or try my hand as an interior designer!

I read an article in *The Times* 02/07/12 on the battle for business between Sindy and Barbie written by Dominic Walsh. He writes that Sindy 'was under threat from her sassier American rival...Barbie was able to tap into the popularity of *Dallas* and *Dynasty*, to establish a foothold that she would not relinquish'. (p.4) Helen Rumbelow points out what is at stake in the battle... it all boils down to the fact that Barbie has no morals...she is the Paris Hilton whereas UK Sindy is the girl next door and is not a plastic bimbo. Natasha Walter in her book *Living Dolls*, censures the pop stars who make raunchy sex videos to promote their music. Recently a local farmer in Bangor, Alan Graham stopped Rihanna from completing her striptease during the filming of her hit, 'We Found Love'. This incident attracted worldwide media attention and ignited a debate on the antics of these pop divas. I may not agree with everything the DUP stands for but I do approve of the farmer's actions.

At the moment, I am reading *War and Peace* and I noticed that when the reader is introduced to Natasha, she is carrying her doll:

> Do you see?... My doll... Mimi... You see... was all Natasha managed to utter (to her everything seemed funny). She leaned against her mother and burst into such a loud, ringing fit of laughter that even the prim visitor could not help joining in. (W&P p. 38)

Later she teases Boris, commenting, 'Kiss the doll'. One moment she is the charming little girl, amusing everyone with her antics and putting on a show with Mimi and the next she is flirting with Boris, and using her doll as prop in her love-making to entice him.

[28] *Things That Make You Feel Cheerful*

Sei speaks of a Yin-Yang master who goes down to the river bed to rid you of a curse. In the notes, McKinney mentions that *harae* or purification was normally associated with the Shinto religion, but was sometimes performed by a Yin-Yang master.

When I studied Zen in San Francisco Zen Centre Paul Haller, my teacher, gave a course on the Sandokai, which means the Harmony of Differences and Same. Paul told us that *san* meant many, *do* meant sameness and *kai* meant harmony. I found this explanation by Zoketsu Norman Fischer, in his website, Every Day Zen:

"San" means all the myriad and differentiated things of this world - all the ordinary things of this world, including not just material things, but also inner things such as thoughts, feelings, and emotions. There is nothing that you could think or experience that isn't distinguished from something else. So the world of distinguishing, the world of mental states, that's the world evoked by "san." And "do" is the opposite. "Do" means oneness, the empty, profound unity of all things. That's the "do" of *Sandokai*. And "kai" means merging, or as Suzuki Roshi explains in his commentary, it actually comes from a root word that means "to shake hands."

參同契 refers to *Cantong qi*, which means, *Kinship of the Three, Akinness of the Three, Triplex Unity, The Seal of the Unity of the Three*. When I studied catechism in primary school, we learned about the Holy Trinity, three persons in one and one in three.

I also enjoy meeting friends in Belfast and having a nice cup of tea with them. My favourite cafés are Sinnamon in Botanic Avenue, Starbucks and Clements Café. Clements was called after Pope Clement VIII, who adored coffee and was responsible for the opening of numerous coffee houses in Rome. Clements' slogan is 'we're religious about coffee.' The term coffee house reminds me of the module I studied while at Queen's University, called 'Satire and Sentiment.' We studied Alexander Pope and Jonathan Swift. During this period famous writers and politicians frequented coffee houses and there was much controversy and debate. In fact not only did Charles II try to close the coffee house, women presented a petition to Parliament to have them closed, as they were taking their husbands away from them. In the 17th and 18th centuries, these places sold alcohol as well as coffee and chocolate. I wrote a poem about Starbucks' café :

There's a Starbucks in Seattle

There's a Starbucks in Seattle
Just right next to Microsoft
Meet me there in an hour

And we'll keep mischief makers and secret agents at bay
You'll want a Caramel Macchiato but will settle for an Americano
as a substitute.
You'll want a chocolate decadence cake but you'll order a marshmallow twizzle as an alternative.
We'll start off by talking about Derrida and Deleuze but we'll listen to Shania Twain instead.

You'll wave to one of your students,
He's writing on Derrida and Deconstruction
You put him right on key concepts, how one expression is dominant and one is derivative,
You have urged him not to conflate post-structuralism with postmodernism, but he does it all the same.
But you'll not want him to approach
Because you won't have something clever to say.
But that's what I like about you,
You're so boring and predictable
And reliable, and pretentious.
It's comforting.

The name Starbucks comes from Starbuck, the chief mate of the Pequod, Ahab's ship in *Moby Dick*.

It is interesting to note that the current logo which stares out from the big coffee mugs was once a mermaid, with a tail, and now it is only a woman's face with long hair, covering the breasts.

I also wrote this poem about Starbucks' mermaid:

Starbucks' Mermaid
Charming Mermaid with quince and comb
grooming her flowing blonde tresses,
hearing the strains of human hymns.
Once she heard them at holy Masses.

She saw the churchwarden's son
Blowing the candles out
and she said 'he is the one'.
In time their love came about.

And one day he left forever
And joined her in the ocean deep.
His mother knew she would never
see her son again and began to weep.

Now in Starbucks,
She becomes the girl next door
Not a mermaid any more.

The other morning I was reading 'The Forsaken Merman' by Matthew Arnold. There is a mermaid legend associated with Zennor, a town in Cornwall.

[29] *A Palm-Leaf Carriage*
This entry makes me think of Sunday drivers who crawl along the motorway at 40 MPH. Most infuriating! I talked to the North West 200 motorbike riders this year. There was a 'meet the driver session' on 16/05/12.

I was fascinated that these young men would do such a dangerous sport. In fact I heard that one of the drivers was killed during the Superstock Race in Portstewart. His name was Mark

Buckley and he came from Loch Lomond in Scotland. He was only thirty-five years old.

On the subject of transport, I think that Nazim Hikmet's poem 'Things I did not Know I Loved' evokes the magic of the train journey. He was travelling on the Prague-Berlin train as night was descending. That sounds so poetic.

Things I Didn't Know I loved

(inspired by Nazim Hikmet's Things I Didn't Know I loved)

Dedicated to Paul Haller, SFZC who read This poem at Benburb Sesshin

It's 2012 March 28th
I'm looking out of the window of the Belfast-Derry train.
The sun is rising.
I never realised how much I liked
This gory orange rising in the East.

I apologise for using this metaphor
But didn't Dickens say we were a rough people.

Near Cloughmills I see ploughed fields.
I love ploughed fields. I never
Actually tilled the land but
Many's a time I heard my father talking about working
The stubborn land round Swatragh with
Horse and plough.

The river Bann means 'white river' and it rises
In the Mournes in the South East and wends its
Way for eighty miles until it reaches the Bann mouth
In the North West. I was born west of the Bann and
Better to have been born east of the Bann
If you want to prosper.

This is the warmest day of spring and the sky is a
Bright blue.
Heaney wrote that the sky was 'a tense diaphragm.'
His sky was the trapped sky at the bottom of the well.
David Bowie sang about the starman waiting in the sky.
Today I am going to reach for the skies.
A man's grasp should exceed his reach. My father said that.

The Zen master once asked me what sky was saying.
I think I failed that question.

I didn't realise how beautiful the trees were. The Douglas
    Firs
At the side of the Frosses Road are English the way oak
Trees are Derry. Charles Lanyon planted the firs on Frosses' bog
In 1839. I want to tie a relic on one of them or take a
    photograph.

The trees are dangerous but no one will hear tell of them
Being cut down.

I love roads especially the A26 which is the main
Road between Antrim and Coleraine. There were
Plans to have a motorway built but they fell through
So the A26 has to take the stress. It is really busy in
The holiday season when cars and caravans travel
In droves to the Coast. Once during the North West 200
Motorbike race I was driving on the A26 and the big bikes
Were riding behind me and almost shadowing me. They
    were
Wraiths out of Lord of the Rings.
They were so eager to pass me and I was glad to see them
    zipping
Off into the distance. The Dunlops were famous motorcyclists
And Joey has a Leisure Centre called after him.
Maybe I just dreamt
That the motorbikes were on my shoulder as I was driving
    because
I was listening to a radio programme about the upcoming
    race.

I remembered how much I love flowers especially roses, red
    roses
Although the dandelions along the roadside are pretty espe-
    cially when
They turn into pretty seed head which resemble spherical
    balls which
We called 'clocks'. It is said you could tell the time of day by
    holding
The 'clock' and blowing on it, saying 'one o'clock, two o'clock,
    etc.

And when there was no little parachute seeds left you knew
    the time.

I love the stars. Joxer says 'Ah, that's the question, that's the
    question
what is the stars?' Catch a falling star and put it in your pocket,
never let it slip away!

I never knew I loved the earth.
I remember driving this stretch of road
One day last January and it was snowing
Heavily. Slemish looked like a pudding
Topped with white sauce Saint Patrick
Must have starved up there with
his sheep for six years.

I never knew I loved the sun.
We see so little of it but it is
Shining today. Hafiz wrote
The sun never says to the earth,
"You owe Me."
But the Aztecs thought they owed the
Sun and many's a heart was ripped
Out and left pulsating in a basin
Under its dazzling rays.

I'm Irish; of course I hate the rain.
George Szirtes said
'Irish rain is slower, heavier.
English rain rarely drenches you'.

We have reached Cullybackey, I will be getting off
When we get to Coleraine. I had bananas in my bag

But I have eaten six squares of chocolate, one
Would have been enough.

I have had to wait fifty seven years to realise
How beautiful the world is.
As the Belfast-Derry train trundles along
anything could happen,
Gatsby could happen.
Gatsby better happen, I'm giving
A lecture on him this morning.

[30] *A Priest Who Gives a Sermon Should be Handsome*

As in many societies, church services can be social as well as religious. Sei comments that the young men leave the sermon after a decent amount of time, and on their way out, 'they throw glances in the direction of the women's carriages and comment to each other'. I remember when I attended mass in the little chapel in Craigavole which I attended in my youth. The priest would always scold people for standing down at the back of the chapel. It was not considered reverent to stand at the back. And sometimes (it was always men) they would slip out during Holy Communion. We were obliged to attend mass every Sunday and go to the sacraments on a regular basis. My grandmother said the rosary every night. I can remember not liking the formality. Although I do recall the benediction of the Blessed Sacrament was very striking. The altar boy would have the charcoal lit in the thurible or incense burner and then pass it to the priest who would swing it a prescribed number of times:

Tantum ergo Sacramentum
Veneremur cernui:
Et antiquum documentum
Novo cedat ritui:

Praestet fides supplementum
Sensuum defectui.

Genitori, Genitoque
Laus et jubilatio,
Salus, honor, virtus quoque
Sit et benedictio:
Procedenti ab utroque
Compar sit laudatio.

Recently I found out that this hymn was the last two verses of a medieval hymn, 'Pange Lingua' which was written by Thomas Aquinas.

I wrote a few lines about the experience:

I recall Benediction of the Blessed Sacrament in Craigavole
    chapel
Sitting in the old wooden pews, in August during a warm
    spell.
The priest in stole and chasuble looks sacrosanct at the start
    of service;
The altar boy tries not to fumble as he prepares the censer
    and adds the incense;
The priest swings the censer a prescribed number of times
    from to right to left
While the congregation bow their heads, preparing to be
    enraptured
As the priest with gold embroidered humeral veil takes the
    monstrance
From where it was placed in splendour, adorned with dahl-
    ias, hydrangeas.
The puffs of frankincense flavoured incense smoke swirl
    about the altar

And fills the aisles, and after the blessing we sing Tantum
  Ergo, probably not
In the best Latin and with all this pomp and ceremony and
  wisps of smoke
From the lovely smell of incense lingering in our noses we
  could just
As easily be in Santiago de Compostela where I heard the
  big Botafumeiro
Swings through the Church like a flying trapeze artist, reach-
  ing the ceiling.

[31] *While I Was Visiting the Bodai Temple*

This excerpt shows Sei's desire to live a more authentic life,
'To be drenched with Lotus dews of Truth' as she attends a sermon on the Salvation Lotus Discourses and a Bodai Temple. She
is capable of more than being dragged into the court intrigues
in which she is immersed.

[32] *The Palace Known as Koshirakawa*

This excerpt shows the way religious events can become like
a mini-court with everyone vying for position. Sei describes the
sumptuary elegance of the ministers, and their elegant clothes,
their lavender gathered trousers and light-blue summer under-
robes. She describes how the court nobles 'were seated just
beyond in a long row above the threshold...next in line behind them were the senior courtiers and young court nobles.'
In Craigavole the two wealthiest families sat in the front pews.

Sei ends the entry with a line from Minamoto no Muneyuki, to
evoke Toshichika's sudden departure from the world. The *Lotus
Discourses* were based on the Buddha Shakyamuni's teachings.
These sutras are the core texts of the Buddhist faith. In the *Lotus
Sutra*, the Buddha emphasised the teaching that we all have
Buddha nature. We all grow old and die and the Buddha gave
people hope that although there is suffering and death, there is

also the extinction of old age and death which can be attained by non-attachment. Sei demonstrates her worldliness by leaving early but she is not going to let Toshichika put her down. His spiritual arrogance in criticising her makes him one of the five thousand whom the Buddha rebuked for thinking they knew it all, and left the teachings early. Sei is certainly a match for the Emperor's nephew.

Somehow this entry made me think of how churches and the army are artificial. Freud commented that 'as a rule a person is not consulted, or is given a choice, as to whether he wants to enter such a group; any attempt at leaving is usually met with persecution or with severe punishment or it has quite definite conditions attached to it.'[10] I was brought up by a deeply religious grandmother who had a profound influence on me. I did resent being forced to make a First Confession and to go into a scary dark confessional box to tell my sins. It was mortifying. We had to learn Catholic catechism off by heart. I will always remember Mrs Johnson explaining what three things were needed in order to commit a mortal sin...full knowledge, full consent and it must be a grievous matter. I see much good in my Catholic faith and I go to Mass each Sunday. However I believe the church is in need of reform, including female ordination. Why should women be discriminated against? It's the highest form of misogyny in the civilised world.

I wrote a modern version of Shakespeare's sonnet 12, 'When I Do Count the Clock That Tells the Time.' It made me realise how good his craft was. I really struggled with it and I am not happy with it:

When I check the time on my wristwatch
I realise this day is nearly over, the roses
That were pink when picked, now wilted
Golden tresses of hair, now grey tinged.
The Horse Chestnut tree in the garden

Which offered me shade, now stripped
All the golden hay which adorned the land
Now cut, baled and stored in silos
This makes me think of your beauty
And how all things are impermanent
When our powers at their greatest
The axe is already waiting to kill
Having an heir might be the only way
To give one a sense of immortality.

[33] *In the Seventh Month When the Heat is Dreadful*
Sei shifts from Lotuses to a more erotic scene; McKinney
comments that she wrote this entry 'in the mode of romantic
tales of the era'. We are given details of the intrigues of a young
woman whose lover has just left her. She imbues the scene with
details of the woman's seductive clothing and how another lover
is enticed when he notices 'the woman's open lattice shutter'.

[34] *Flowering Trees*
This entry references the tragic tale of the Chinese Emperor
Xuanzong and his concubine Yang Guifei. Because of his obses-
sion with her, he neglects his duties and this leads to a mutiny.
That reminded me of a play I did at Queen's, called *Edward II*
by Christopher Marlowe, in which the King's dalliance with Piers
Gaveston, leads to tragic consequences for both of them. I studied
'Loveliest of Trees' at school. It was written by A.E. Houseman:

Loveliest of trees, the cherry now
Is hung with bloom along the bough,
And stands about the woodland ride
Wearing white for Eastertide.

Now, of my three score years and ten,
Twenty will not come again,

And take from seventy springs a score,
It only leaves me fifty more.

And since to look at things in bloom
Fifty springs are little room,
About the woodlands I will go
To see the cherry hung with snow

I took this photograph of a tree in bloom this spring. It might be an apple blossom. It was taken outside Newtownabbey Further Education College.

I grew up in a farm in south Derry and I heard my father referring to 'fairy trees' or 'gentle bushes'...these were in fact the whitethorn which were sacred to the 'little folk.'But I do know that I would not cut down a fairy bush, in fact none of the farmers in our townland would. My father told me that a man needed more space in his field and he decided to cut down a few of the fairy trees. He had hardly put the axe to the first tree when, he was struck by lightning. My father said it put the fear of God in everyone. Since that, no one would ever dare cut down their fairy trees. In a neighbouring parish there was a story told about a man who became the new owner of a farm where a huge fairy tree was located. The farmer had ploughed around it but never interfered with it. The new farmer was fed up with this situation and he ordered his farm hand to cut it down. However the farm hand said he was too afraid to do the tree any harm, as he put it. The new farmer took a huge axe and cut the tree down himself. He got up the next day and cut the wood for firewood. "See" he said to the farm hand, "I'm none the worse for the wear."' But over the next few years a series of calamities befell him. After his youngest child died in a freak accident, he decided to sell the farm and move away. He said, "although I hate to admit it, I believe this place is haunted. I have only one child left and I cannot afford to lose him as well." The new farmer that took over planted a new tree as soon as he moved in and he never endured anything but good luck.

It is interesting how folklore grows up around trees, and in Ireland the whitethorn tree is linked to the fairy tradition. I once heard that after the Tuatha de Danann disappeared, they became the little people and went underground. However not all people in the North of Ireland would agree with fairy lore. Because of the Catholic/Protestant divide, two distinct heritages exist. This was recently highlighted in a debate in the Northern Ireland Assembly on 13/04/12 when a DUP MLA interjected in a debate over an event known as 'An Irish Homecoming'. Mrs D Kelly called on the Executive to support the Irish Tourist Board in promoting this event. Mr Stephen Moutray had other ideas:

'To my mind, next year's "An Irish Homecoming" will be hugely sentimental and very Irish in a way that I cannot and will not really identify with. It is a sort of "Mother Ireland" concept that conjures up images of leprechauns, shillelaghs, pints of Guinness, donkeys, dancing at the crossroads and thatched cottages. In other words, it is the sort of stuff that we see far too much of in retail outlets at our airports.'

So one man's idea of culture is another man's idea of caricature. Recently I reviewed *The Beauty Queen of Leenane*, which overturned the stereotype of Mother Ireland and white washed thatched cottages:

However scene-by-scene, McDonagh strips away these pretensions to give us a menacing and ultimately murderous depiction of the reality behind this dysfunction. This is not the Tourist Board's board image of the idyllic west of thatched cottages and homely maidens, but a hard-hitting depiction of a community strangled almost literally by the repressive mores of a post-1922 Republic, riddled with mass emigration and poverty, both monetary and emotional.

[35] *Ponds*
This entry where Sei refers to the drowning maiden, 'her hair tangled as in sleep'. This reminded me of Gertrude's description of Ophelia's death from *Hamlet* :

When down her weedy trophies and herself
Fell in the weeping brook. Her clothes spread wide;
And, mermaid-like, awhile they bore her up:
Which time she chanted snatches of old tunes; (*Hamlet 4, 7)*

Ophelia's death is one of the most poignant in literature.

[36] *Seasonal Palace Festivals*
The description of the seasonal palace festival is very evocative and Sei conjures up a bygone aesthetic. She has a condescending attitude to the 'little lower-class girls' and the houses of common folk. Japanese society was clearly permeated with imperial pomp. One cannot help criticising their pretensions but at the same time valuing the way they celebrated nature. I recall being a flower girl at a Corpus Christi procession and I had a basket of flower petals which I dropped along the route. I remember my friend being rather prodigal with her petals and she had run out before she reached the chapel porch. The teacher scooped into my basket and gave her some. I always knew I was a thrifty person. There's a parable in the Bible about the

wise and foolish bridesmaids who are to attend the bridegroom when he arrives. The wise ones have enough oil in their lamps whereas the foolish ones run out. I hope that I am careful to observe the tenets of my faith and not waste my precious time.

[37] *Trees that Have no Flowers*

This beautifully written extract honours the magic and beauty of trees. The county where I was born is Derry, *doire* in Irish, meaning oak. The oak tree was sacred to the Druids. We still have the superstition of 'touching wood' for luck and this may stem from our Druidic heritage. Sei mentions the leaves of the yuzuriha which were used to hold food for the dead. In the Celtic tradition the people lit bonfires at Samhain and left out food offerings for the dead. On All Soul's we were permitted a plenary  indulgence if we went to Confession and received the Blessed Sacrament and then paid a visit to a cemetery. The church collects lists of the deceased in the parish and offers up masses for their eternal souls. In Buddhism there are Hungry Ghost ceremonies. My teacher, Paul Haller, performed one of these ceremonies this August in Tassahara, chanting , "We hear your cries of hunger and make these offerings to feed your bodies and free your souls."

[38] *Birds*

This entry contains many charming observances on birds. The image of the mandarin ducks brushing the frost from each other's wings is delightful. She always praises the *hototogisu* liberally but laments that despite drawing attention to itself with its distinctive cuckoo call, it tends to hide among the orange trees.

I could never capture on paper how much I admire birds. Sometimes as I sit reading in my study in Kansas Avenue, I hear swans flying over my house. W.B. Yeats in his famous poem 'The Wild Swans at Coole' speaks of the magnificent nine and fifty swans whose hearts have not grown cold:

I took this picture at a garden centre in Warrenpoint

> All's changed since I,
>   hearing at twilight,
> The first time on this
>   shore,
> The bell-beat of their wings above my head,
> Trod with a lighter tread.

I wrote 'Swan Upping,' a meditation on the 'Troubles':

While this flurry of activity takes place
and the innocent birds submit with grace
to the annual upping, on the Thames,
the swans in the Waterworks in north Belfast
move smoothly along,
on the upper lake,
just as they have always done despite
the six hundred slayings that took place
in the warren of streets.

At the height of the tit-for-tat
people were picked at random
and roughly put to death.
No royal prerogative,
no time for goodbyes

no last anointing
no viaticum.

But on this warm July afternoon,
as these mythical birds surrender to
their annual upping
or glide along majestically
upon the upper lake, in North Belfast,
they conjure up a folk tale,
where Siegfried and Odette
and live happily ever after.

[39] *Refined and Elegant Things*
This entry reminds me of a line from the *Sandokai* or
Harmony of Difference and Equality:

Refined and common speech come together in the dark,
Clear and murky phrases are distinguished in the light.

[40] *Insects*
I like butterflies most of all. I wrote a poem about butterflies
booming on bombsites:

David Bellamy recalled
A curious fact:
Flower seeds
Fell from enemy bomb-bays
Along with the shells, and
London saw another
Unintended consequence of war:
Flowers blossomed on the
Bombsites, and there was
A excess of
Red Admirals,

Small Tortoiseshells,
Orange Tips,
Painted Ladies,
and Brimstones

In July, I volunteered at the Peace Camp installation at Whitepark Bay. It was an extraordinary experience. Instead of staring at my computer screen and googling everything under the sun, I was able to look out at the endless horizon and imagine sea myths, sea creatures and even mermaids. There are many types of butterflies in this area, including Small Heath, the Dark Green Fritillary, the Orange Tip, and the Common Blue. There is also a rare species known as Wood White.

[41] *In the Seventh Month the Wind Blows Hard*
We are coming into the autumn. I am back teaching at college. The day goes so quickly. I have very little time to reflect, though I did notice that the leaves blew on to my bonnet as I drove out of Belfast this morning, I have also noticed that little clumps of leaves do reels and jigs on the pavement. September is the harvest month. I wrote this yesterday after doing a poetry workshop in Slemish College:

A woman stares at the pineapples in Tesco's Ballymena
As in a trance
She reaches out and lifts one and says,
'are you the one?'
A woman with a little girl placed in the trolley
A pink mademoiselle in pigtails
Is tempted by tangerines.
An old man stands in a daze
Mesmerised by melons
He picks one and holds it for a moment,
Then moves to loose onions.

A chap is captivated by carrots.
An old woman is tempted by a turnip.
The sales assistant arrives to tidy
The parsnips, they're a mess.

[42] *Unsuitable Things*

Once again Sei exposes her condescension to the 'common people' when she remarks that it is unsuitable when snow falls on their houses. I am reminded of the democratic words of the Bible which reads the rain falls on the just and the unjust. She does not even think they are worthy of having the moonlight shine on them. She also condemns older women for getting pregnant. This is quite topical as almost every woman's magazine debates motherhood. There is always a glut of prevailing knowledge on everything from mums' behaviour at the school gate to her ovaries. Her condemnation of the toothless old crone as she screws up her face to eat sour plums is very witty, if a little intolerant. I know some people who cannot bear anyone eating beside them, especially if there are devouring crisps or apples. I was in the Opera House recently and people were eating beside me. Also in the cinema people carry in buckets of popcorn and what doesn't get munched finishes up squashed into the floor. I was told that ladies do not eat in the public street but as I walk down Royal Avenue, Belfast, people are often eating and drinking. It's a 'to go' culture.

It is unsuitable to wear bright colours to funerals but I am sure there are societies where this is not the case. On a personal level, I do not like rude people, or as Max Erhmann's poem *Desiderata* advocates,

Go placidly amidst the noise and haste, and remember what peace there may be in silence. As far as possible without surrender be on good terms with all persons.

Speak your truth quietly and clearly; and listen to others, even the dull and the ignorant; they too have their story.

Avoid loud and aggressive persons, they are vexatious to the spirit. If you compare yourself with others, you may become vain or bitter; for always there will be greater and lesser persons than yourself.

[43] *A Lot of us are Gathered in the Long Room*
This sounds as if Sei enjoyed these interactions and does not like anyone to be a killjoy in this instance. I love a good chat myself. As a peripatetic teacher, I have no opportunity for these kinds of chats any more but I recall that when I worked in the public sector, I was good friends with a bunch of girls and we were renowned for our caustic wit. This is an excerpt from my short story, 'Travelling Home':

You could see the bosses talking in this meeting room, which had huge windows and everyone called it the fish bowl. However the windows did not open, giving it a claustrophobic atmosphere. The office was open plan and you could observe all the comings and goings. One time a friend of Julie's came into the office and told her it was an unreal place. People seemed as if they were zombies; they got up from their desk and walked about as if they had been heavily medicated. It was as if no one had any energy. She said it was freaky. Maybe the whole open plan office was one huge bell jar, where the air had been vacuumed out. Word filtered through from the fish bowl which Julie now referred to as the 'bell jar' office that there was some big thing on about new commissioning arrangements and budgets. When the meeting was over, Julie popped her head into Celia's office and said, "Hi Celia, have you heard any more word about my transfer?" The senior accountant looked at Julie and said "These things take time." And then added, "you know once I was in a post and I wanted out, so I just applied for another job."

[44] *No Menial Position Could be Finer than that of Palace Groundswomen*

McKinney points out that the position of groundswomen was a much coveted post in this period. They were responsible for carrying messages. These days the position of courier would not be a prestigious job. And there are so many ways to communicate electronically, and even video conferencing. I use Facebook and some of the modern social media. But part of me would like to go back to writing letters and use more old fashioned means of communication. In *Antony and Cleopatra*, the messengers from Rome intrude upon the Antony's self-indulgent life in Egypt. In the days before telephones and telegraphs, no doubt these messengers were necessary for conveying information.

[45] *Amongst the Serving Men's Positions*

I suppose the modern equivalent of that would be a valet. In the film *Mrs Brown* Billy Connolly plays the role of the real life John Brown who became Queen Victoria's favourite after the death of her beloved husband. His position within the royal household was that of equerry. He became an object of jealousy because of the Queen's regard for him. The way courts are set up can create an unhealthy atmosphere of favouritism and back biting which is not healthy.

[46] *Secretary Controller Yukinari*

In this entry Sei shows her ability to cross swords and intellectually engage with Yukinari. The teasing and flirtatious behaviour is a joy to read. When she quotes from Morosuke, he retorts with a line from Bo Jiyu and she pulls out a Confucian maxim. He appreciates her wit and looks beyond the superficiality of her make-up.

I read an article in the *Belfast Telegraph* (25/10/12) today about Paddy McGurgan, the most famous make-up artist in the world. I cut out the picture of one of his creations. One of my students said her daughter did the same. I do not wear much makeup. A man I know has multiple sclerosis, a very serious neurological disease. He said he loves it when his carers come in the morning, wearing makeup and that it puts him in a good mood, whereas if they descend upon him like harbingers from hell he is deflated. My aunt Mary who is over ninety says she never wore makeup. She said she never needed a top dressing.

[47] *Horses*

I always look up at horses grazing at Donegore as I drive down the M2 toward Antrim. They always strike me as exquisite creatures. I wrote a short story about a horse called Black Bob. I heard the story in a writers' group in Comber about this famous horse who died of a broken heart after his master was killed by the Ghurkhas.

If you think we stop or falter
While in the fray we're gin'
Just watch the steps with our heads erect,
While our band plays "Garryowen."

Black Bob had not a clue where Cherryvalley townland was and he had never heard of Comber, County Down. Horses, like Holden Caulfield never want the 'David Copperfield kind of crap'—where their masters were born, or if they had unhappy childhoods or if they had any brothers or sisters and Black Bob was no exception to this rule.

All horses want to know is if their masters will distinguish themselves for if they are the heroes, their horses
will partake of their good fortune. This is the sort of
David Copperfield they relate to. And heroes' horses are
always at the front of the parade. So forgive Black Bob
if he were not in the faintest bit interested in the bi-
ography of his beloved master, Hugh Rollo Gillespie,
K.C.B.1776-1814.

I watched *Gulliver's Travels* today. It was a mini-series
starring Ted Danson. This production was true to the spirit of the book. I thought the depiction of the Yahoos and
the Houyhnhnms was excellent. I live beside the Cave Hill
Mountain, which was the inspiration for Swift's Gulliver. In
1695 Swift came north from Dublin after taking Holy Orders
and was appointed as Prebend of Kilroot. There were two other churches in this parish, in Ballynure and Templecorran. It is
said that at this time County Antrim was mainly Presbyterian
and that the Established Church had few adherents. Swift spent
two miserable winters in Kilroot, but I am sure it was a fer-
tile breeding ground for his literary imagination. In profile it
looks like the head of a giant. I remember studying *Gulliver's
Travels* at Queen's University in the early nineties. The course
was entitled, 'Satire and Sentiment'. We studied Pope and Swift
mostly. I enjoyed reading these authors as I had never studied
them before. Pope's *Rape of the Lock* was an impressive mock
epic. Hampton Court Palace was a place which encompassed
the sublime and the ridiculous, a place where Queen Anne,
"dost sometimes counsel take—and sometimes tea". This was
an example of zeugma, a figure of speech where one word is
applied to two adjacent words but is appropriate only to one
of them. Another example is from Dickens; "Mr Pickwick took
his hat and his leave."

[48] *Oxen*

There is an expression, 'as strong as an ox.' We refer to cows as cattle in Northern Ireland. A farmer might say, 'I am going out to look at the cattle'. My grandmother said that when the cattle gather together in the corner of the field, there was going to be a thunderstorm. My father was a dairy farmer. Every day when I was growing up, I remember him bringing in an aluminium bucket of milk, still warm from the milking. The ox is an important symbol in Zen, representing the mind. In the Ten Oxherding Pictures, the ox herder sets out to find the ox. First of all he can only see its tracks, but at least he has set out on his journey to enlightenment. Over a period of time he sees the ox, captures it, and after a hard struggle, he tames it. This means that the student commits his life to his practice and awakens his Buddha nature. He rides the ox home. After a period he has achieved no-mind and he has returned to his original nature. He re-enters the market and is able to teach others.

[49] *Cats*

Sei says cats should be very black, except for their bellies which should be white. Black cats are supposed to be lucky.

My friend Joyce with whom I stay two nights in Coleraine has a cat. It is called Le Roi/ Leroy. It is a tabby cat… with distinctive striations on his coat and a distinguishing 'm' on his forehead. When I was learning my lines for the part of Lady Catherine de Burgh, I  practised in Joyce's garden. Sometimes Le Roi would perform as well…dancing with Joyce. Once Le Roi sent me a text to my HTC phone:

Bonjour Lady Catherine. Thank you for the very special card that you kindly sent me. I love it. Your acting abilities impressed me in the garden and my mam says that you might do your part again when you come to visit me. I've just had my second lunch, a sachet of pilchards, which is quite nice. I stayed out all last night and so was hungry this morning. Mam says she is going to tell Wally about your performance in the Crescent.

À bientôt

Le Roi

In Case 14 of the Mumonkan or Gateless Gate, monks from the eastern and western halls were quarrelling over the owner-ship of a cat. Nansen lifts the cat and says, 'If you can give an answer I will save the cat, if not I will kill it.' No one answers and he cuts the cat in two. When Joshu returned in the evening, Nansen related the incident to him. Joshu removed his sandal, put it on his head  and walked out. Nansen said if Joshu had have been there, the cat would not have died. This koan never made sense to me until I heard a Zen teacher explaining that it was about the fundamental truth. Life and death is every moment. Cutting the cat in two reminds me of the story in the Bible when the two women who both claim to be the mother of a baby; they ask Solomon to decide who the real one is. Solomon, asks for a knife and threatens to cut the baby in two. The true mother is horrified at this prospect and offers to relinquish the baby. Then Solomon knows she is the real mother. In the same way, the monks did not care about the fate of the cat, but rather who owned it. In Belfast there have been protests over the decision not to fly the Union Jack for 365 days over the City Hall. The protesters have blocked roads, intimidated the Alliance Party and so forth, just because they disagree with the decision. Conflict arises when one person says, this is my country, my flag and if you disagree with my worldview, I am going to flatten you. Like the monks in the monastery, fighting over something petty and forgetting their real purpose.

I took this picture during the flag protests...wouldn't it be great if we could 'swim between the flags'

[50] *Carriage Runners*

Sei would have enjoyed the Bond films with their trim muscular good looking male leads. She makes no secret of her aesthetic regarding the physical makeup of her carriage runners. Carriage runners and escort guards should be trim, slightly on the thin side.

Once again Sei puts her aesthetic values above her human values in wishing the carriage runners should not be overweight. This entry reminded me of a film, *Lady Caroline Lamb*, (1972) directed by Robert Bolt. I will never forget the scene where Lady Caroline, played by Sarah Miles, has become completely infatuated with the romantic poet Lord Byron. In one of the scenes, at the height of her obsession, she takes the place of one of Lord Byron's carriage runners and shocks the guests at the Wellington dinner. I saw this some time ago but it impressed me deeply. How could anyone humiliate themselves so much? And yet there was something magnificent in the gesture. Today, she might be classed as a stalker.

CHAPTER THREE:

Things That Cannot be Compared

[51] *Page Boys*
Page boys and ring bearers are sometimes part of a modern wedding ceremony. They will normally be dressed in a similar suit to the bridegroom and they usually look really cute. Billy Lowther-Pinkerton and Tom Pettifer were the two page boys at Prince William and Kate's wedding.

[52] *Ox Handlers*
Sei even has an opinion on the physical make up of ox handlers. She also wishes them to be clever looking, for some unknown reason.

[53] *The Mighty Roll Call*
This sounds like an ideal opportunity for the ladies-in-waiting to spy on the senior courtiers and to hear them call out their names. This could either pique interest or provoke dread, depending on whether the courtier was a current suitor or a former devotee, best forgotten. Paul Muldoon wrote a poem called 'Anseo' which explored the theme of violence during the 'Troubles' where the roll call carried out by the primary school teacher was later replicated by an IRA leader's military roll call.

When the master was calling the roll
At the primary school in Collegelands,
You were meant to call back Anseo
And raise your hand
As your name occurred.

I met up with a few of my school friends a few years ago. Joanne was able to do the roll call. I was amazed. I wrote this poem in response to the reunion.

Loreto Convent Reunion 4th August 2008

I saw them driving into the car park in The Lodge Park Hotel.
They were in a black shiny car, wearing Rayban glasses.
They had become the teachers we used to deride 35 years
    ago.
I had become the same minus the Raybans.
Joanne had perfect recall for the roll call:
Allen
Breen
Kearney
Lagan
McKenna
McCaughan
McGrath
McKeague
McKinney
Mullan.

[54] *It's Disgusting When a Well-Bred Young Man Casually Calls Out the Name of Some Low-ranking Woman he's Visiting*

Once again, Sei reiterates her desire to keep up appearances. Etiquette is still deeply embedded in the Japanese culture. When I visited Tokyo a few years ago with a group of Americans, we were told to be respectful while using the public transport as sometimes Japanese people meditate while travelling. Also our tour guide told us that Japan was not a 'back-slapping culture'.

These reflections on manners and what is appropriate in so-cial discourse would seem somewhat dated now but I suppose there is still a measure or a modicum of propriety left in society. I have seen parents correcting their children for pointing and for shouting out loudly. But behaviour is not so highly regulated in these post feudal days. Although as far as I am aware, you have to call a doctor, Doctor and a consultant, Mr. In the COE you address the bishop as my Lord, and a minister as Reverend Smith. You address the Queen as Your Majesty on first meeting her and afterwards as Ma'am. In this excerpt it is not made clear if he is calling on his lover. McKinney states that there is no suspicion that the man is calling on her as her lover.

[55] *Young People and Babies should be Plump.*

The health gurus all tell us now that babies should not be over fed. Most western countries are in the middle of an obesity crisis. One in five people in Northern Ireland is obese. Lack of exercise, bad diet. Not enough roughage.

[56] *Little Children Waving Quaint Toy Bows*

Sei is not usually so maternal and it was nice to see this aspect of her personality. I am just back at work after my Christmas break and during this period I saw children rushing out of their houses to show off their presents. I noticed a brother and a sister trying out new bikes. A friend of mine was telling me that he wanted to buy his eight year old son an iPad for Christmas. He did not want an iPad...he wanted a laptop...which was duly bought for him. But he never bothered with it. Then (I was somewhat amazed at this stage), my friend said that he topped up his Xbox. An Xbox is a video game console. Akio Mori, a Japanese professor commented, 'Many video games stir up tension and a feeling of fear, and there is a very real concern that this could have a long-term effect on the autonomic nerves.' An iPad according to the advertisement 'is thin, it is beautiful, there is no right way or wrong way, it is crazy powerful, it's magical, you already know how to use it, it's 200,000 aps and counting and it's only a revolution just begun'. My friend told me that his six year-old daughter was delighted with her new doll and new updated doll's house which has a kitchen. She still believes in Santa. That's the only magic left in their house, my friend said.

So gone are the days when little children wave quaint toy bows. Although yesterday in Debenhams' café I noticed a few young children with cuddly toys that squeaked.

[57] *The Central Gate of a Grand House Lies Open*

I took this picture of Sperrin sheep on my way to Strabane. It was a beautiful September morning.

In south Belfast there are some beautiful houses. I noticed some the other day in Piney Hills. It is amazing to see the beautiful driveways and the landscaped gardens. I attended my teaching degree graduation recently and it was held in Tullyglass House Hotel. I took a picture of a beautiful sculpture of a lion outside the front door.

[58] *Waterfalls*

The notion of the Cloistered Emperor attending the Furu Falls conjures up a bygone era of the idyllic Heian period. There are famous waterfalls in Glenariff Forest Park. The main trees in the forest are Sitka spruce but there are some Douglas fir and some Japanese larch. There is a famous poem called 'The Stolen Child,' by W.B. Yeats which is one of the most haunting poems I ever read. I visited Glencar Waterfall in County Leitrim (near Sligo) which was the setting for the poem. Waterfalls, it is said, are magical places where the natural world meets the supernatural:

Come away, O human child!
To the waters and the wild
With a faery, hand in hand,
For the world's more full of weeping than you can understand.

This beautiful refrain is echoed throughout the poem.

[59] *Rivers*

Rivers have always been the subject of many famous poems. Heraclitus of Ephesus said that we cannot stand in the same river twice. This is echoed in the poem Sei refers to
where one moment the river is
deep and the next it is shallow. Impermanence. I hate the
smallest change to my routine.
On Monday 14th January, I
went to the train station in
Yorkgate, at 6.55am — that's
the time it leaves for Coleraine. The next stop is Mossley West,
then Antrim, Ballymena, Cullbackey, Coleraine. The names
come across the PA system with a reassuring familiarity. But to
my horror the timetable had changed. I looked up at a notice
in the train station (which is just a shelter really and quite in-
hospitable) and it said 'New Train schedule to take effect from
6/01/13'. The River Bann in Coleraine is a beautiful river. I
took this photograph recently.

It looks idyllic.

[60] *I Do Wish Men, When They're Taking Their Leave from a Lady at Dawn, Wouldn't Insist on Adjusting their Clothes to a Nicety*

Sei's comments on her desire to have the lovers' part in a
tasteful way. She is a true romantic. Her views are quite liberal

considering the norms of Classical Japanese culture. The court seemed to be a hub of intrigues, and secret assignations. In Sei's view a tastefully choreographed departure trumps anything else.

[61] *Bridges*

There is a beautiful bridge over the River Bann. Painters often paint bridges. John Lavery, a famous Irish painter, painted a stone bridge in Grez.

[62] *Villages*

I was born in the townland of Crossland, two miles outside the village of Swatragh. The word Swatragh comes from the Irish 'suaitreach' meaning 'billeted soldier.'

[63] *Plants*

Sei brings the plants to life and her description of the plantain is interesting. She tells us the word *omodaka* means uplifted face. She imagines this plant to be a person with his nose stuck up in the air. The rose mallow she informs us makes you feel it has more intelligence than a real plant.

The Irish for scarlet pimpernel is Falcaire Fiain and is also known as Seamair Mhuire which means Virgin Mary's Shamrock. It was believed to have magical powers, and could enable a person to understand what birds and animals were saying to each other.

[64] *Flowering Plants*

In the spring, I love to see the rhododendron in bloom. I remember learning how to spell rhododendron in primary school. On the same day I learned to spell hippopotamus and somehow I connect the two words.

[65] *Poetry Anthologies*

Famous publishing houses for poetry are Faber and Faber. I have published some poetry in local anthologies, for example, Shalom Writers Group and Forward Poetry.

At the moment I am preparing poems to enter in a few competitions. I quite like to respond to prompts set by the competition panel, for example a recent one set the topic of 'the end of the year'.

[66] *Poetic Topics*

What topic is not poetical? I am sure every topic could be rendered into a poetical theme in the hands of a skilful poet. I listen to the radio each morning and so often the news items contain poetic language.

For example the announcer this morning talked about snow on the motorways and main roads. This phrase contains alliteration.

I took this picture from the 5th Floor in the tower block of the Northern Regional College, December 2010.

[67] *Disturbing Things*

She mentions the mother of a monk who has gone on a twelve-year retreat.

I am a Zen student in the Soto tradition. My teacher comes from San Francisco Zen Centre. I heard that once you become an ordained priest you have to live in the Zen Centre for three years. That makes sense as in a way you have entered practice... you have made a commitment.

In class we discussed horror films today. One of the students is going to do a review of *Saw*. She googled a clip. This weird guy on a bike. He look like an diabolical clown.

[68] *Things that cannot be Compared*
She use binaries of night and day, summer and winter.

Fast and slow
Fat and thin
Round and square
War and peace
Serious and funny
Comedy and tragedy
Storm and calm
Baby and adult
Save and spend
Loss and find
Diet and gorge
Speech and silence
Penny pinching and spendthrift
Morning and night
Truth and lies
Marriage and divorce
Mouse and lion
Confidence and insecurity
Employment and unemployment
Fidelity and infidelity
Industry and sloth
Lust and renunciation
Allotment and field
Eagle and sparrow
Spruce branches laden with snow
Sun melting the ice

[69] *Summer Provides the Most Delightful Setting for a Secret Assignation*
There is something romantic about a winter romance. *Dr Zhivago* had many scenes shot in a winter landscape.

[70] *A Man Comes Calling, Perhaps for Some Intimate Conversation*
There must have been so many illicit affairs and intrigues in the Imperial Court. In this media saturated day, where people document their every waking moment, and everyone is blogging and tweeting, I think we have lost a sense of intimacy.

[71] *Rare Things*
Orchids are valuable because they are rare. We hear about a rare art collection or a rare book collection. Queen's University Belfast has a special collection of books published between 1475 and 1700. There are also six volumes donated by Judge Mitchell in 1840 which are:

a Latin Bible (1592)
a Greek New Testament (1760)
a French New Testament (1664)
a Greek lexicon (1821)
a copy of Locke's Essay concerning Human Understanding (1760) in two volumes

[72] *Our Apartments in the Long Room.*
I like the notion of women's quarters.

[73] *When Her Majesty Was in Residence*
The Japanese have a deep connection to nature. Sei's reference to moon gazing emphasises that. The momiji-gari custom of going out to the forest to gaze at the autumn leaves began in this period.

Such pomp. I heard that Queen Elizabeth re-introduced the order of dignity. Kate Middleton should bow to Prince Beatrice because she is a commoner.

[74] *Things Later Regretted*
This morning I had to drive from Belfast to collect a few more files that I needed to complete a sample for cross marking. I was quite annoyed as I was sure I had taken the right amount yesterday.

[75] *Things that Look Enjoyable*
A walk in the park...seeing cygnets...the buds appearing.

[76] *The Day after the Litany of Buddha Names*
Great reverence was shown for these feasts.

[77] *When Secretary Captain Tadanobu Heard Certain Baseless and Ridiculous Rumours That Were Circulating Concerning Me*
Sei never fails to amuse her readers with these anecdotes of her court intrigues.

[78] *The Following Year, Towards the End of the Second Month*
In this excerpt Tadanobu in his 'gorgeous damask cloak in the cherry blossom combination' is the personification of a Byronic hero.

[79] *When One's Returned Home on a Visit.*
Me kuwase...as McKinney points out, this expression contains a pun for it both means 'make you eat seaweed' and 'send you a silent message with the eyes.'
Sei's antics in this passage, where she uses a piece of seaweed to communicate her feelings, touches on the melodramatic.

And it is reminiscent of some the histrionics the pop and film stars indulge in. A name that seems to be in the paper is Taylor Swift...an American pop star. One minute she's in a relationship with Harry Styles, another mega pop star and the next, it's all off and she's in Richard Branson's hot tub along with another young blonde socialite.

This is an image of the sun setting at Cultra, outside Holywood, Count Down, July 2013.

[80] *Things that Create the Appearance of Deep Emotion*

Once I remember feeling very emotional after watching a production of *Othelllo*. My father's last illness in January 2005 was a very sad occasion. The day I heard he had gone into hospital, I was walking along the west strand in Portrush. As my sister was communicating the news, I remember looking out at a surfer who seem to be surfing very far out near dangerous rocks. I remember thinking that was a metaphor for my father's life. Taking too many risks, swimming far out beyond the pale.

[81] *After Our Visit to the Guard Office*

The fact that Sei can be summoned by the empress, reminds the reader that her intrigues are constantly monitored and that she is answerable for her behaviour and comments. I would be very anxious if I were called to account for my actions. Being summoned by a higher authority can be anxiety-provoking.

[82] *Once When her Majesty was in Residence*

This reference to continuous sutra reading reminds me of how fervent some of the Buddhist practices can be. Sei's attitude to the itinerant nun is typical of her lack of compassion. In Belfast we see migrants Selling the *Big Issue*. One lady sits outside the bakery on a Saturday morning at the Fortwilliam shops. I always give her some money.

The fall of snow and the building of the snow mountain reminds me of the snow we had recently. While I was driving with the utmost care, young people were building snow men and sleighing down the slope at the roundabout beside Corr's Corner Hotel. Tarrantino's *Django Unchained* has a scene where Django uses a snowman for target practice.

[83] *Splendid Things*
A family gathering. I attended my nephew's birthday party today. My three sisters were there. My grand nieces were there. Orlagh had a little black horse called Angus and a doll with red hair. I helped them to put twelve candles on Jake's cake.

[84] *Things of Elegant Beauty*
A swan. A ballet dancer.
We have a poinsettia in the Zen Centre which had the most dazzling red leaves.

[85] *When Her Majesty Provided the Gosechi Dancers*
Recently I watched *Strictly Come Dancing* in my friend Joyce's house. A comment was made, 'the audience does not realise how much power it has.' Kyle Minogue sang 'Do the Locomotive.' It was goodbye to Richard and Erin, two of the dancers.

[86] *Another Elegant Sight*
Another elegant thing is a beautifully laid dining room table. You see them in period costume dramas.

[87] *At the Time of the Gosechi Festival*
There are lots of festivals in Belfast. There are literary festivals. There was a Charles Dickens literary festival in Belfast 2012. Dickens visited Belfast in August 1858. He said, 'Belfast was a fine place with a rough people.'

[88] *One Day Her Majesty Brought along a Bewa called Nameless*
It is a wonderful custom to name a musical instrument. In a book by P. Delfabbro, and A. H. Winefield, I read that regular gamblers often personify their slot machines.

[89] *I Remember an Occasion*
Sei's praise of her mistress is effusive. We cannot possibly replicate this aesthetic. What a cultured and educated court!

[90] *Infuriating Things*
Getting a parking ticket is the most infuriating thing imaginable. I got one a few weeks ago...I was parked in Academy Street, just outside the Zen Centre. I also hate it when a shop assistant refuses to sell me an out-of-date sandwich. I picked up one yesterday in Tesco's filling station. But it was one day out of date. There was another packet of sandwiches there but it had three in it and it cost £1.55. In the end she sold me a pack if three for £1 because it was dated 27/11/13 which was the current date.

[91] *Things it's Infuriating and Embarrassing to Witness*
I personally do not like crude remarks. There are so many interesting words in the language...why use crude ones? The word crude comes from the Latin *crudus*/raw or rough.

[92] *Startling and Disconcerting Things*
When driving the other day on the M5, the rain was lashing down. I had just driven back from Ballymena and I was heading to my Gestalt Class. The cars up ahead slowed down suddenly and I was worried that that I would run into the car in front and not get stopped in time. I should have been driving more cautiously in such dreadful weather.

[93] *Regrettable Things*
Je ne regrette rien.

[94] *At the Time of the Abstinence and the Prayer of the Fifth Month*
Lent began on Ash Wednesday 13th February, 2013. It started really early this year. When I was young Lent was a hard six weeks without sweets. I really missed them. On Shrove Tuesday, I was teaching English to my ESOL class. I heard about the festivals in Catholic countries. For example the Shrove Tuesday festival in Brazil is called 'Fat Tuesday'. These festivals are also called 'Mardi Gras'. People dress in masquerade and parade through the streets. It is a colourful spectacle.

[95] *It was while we were in the Office of the Empress's Household*
There are still some castles left in Ireland, for example Carrickfergus Castle. Also there is a famous castle in Fermanagh, called Crom Castle. It is owned by Lord Erne, whose father was equerry to King George VI. Lord Erne inherited the castle in 1939, when he was a child of two after his father had been killed in WW2. At the moment the TV programme
'*Blandings*' is being filmed there, with famous actors such as Timothy Spall and Jennifer Saunders. The estate, surrounded by Lough Erne, has boathouses, cottages and the oldest yew trees in Ireland.

[96] *There Was a Large and Distinguished Gathering*
This witty interchange between Her Majesty and Sei, show how high spirited the court was. Each gathering was an occasion for a display of verbal dexterity.

[97] *The Emperor Paid a Visit*
Liam Neeson, the greatest actor ever to leave these shores is receiving the freedom of Ballymena today. Today's film stars are the new royalty.

[98] *One Wet Day During the Endless Rains*
On Saturday night the rain beat against the skylight window like hungry ghosts trying to get in.

[99] *There Could Have Been no more Splendid Celebrations Conceivable*
The preparations that went into to hosting this royal visit were amazing. The detail which Sei furnishes us with is extraordinary, from the description of 'Her Majesty's two plum-pink cloaks…draped over three scarlet robes of glossed silk' to the ablutions and not forgetting the mat that was rolled out and the temporary bridgeway.

[100] *A Branch of Plum from which the Blossoms had Fallen*
Sei's remarkable wit is the talk and envy of the court.

CHAPTER FOUR:

Things that Look Ordinary but Become Extraordinary when Written

[101] *Around the End of the Second Month*
There was terrible storm in Ireland on 5th January 1839, known as 'oiche na gaoithe moire' which means 'night of the big wind'. Many lives were lost and much property was destroyed.

[102] *Things that have Far to Go*
They say that Thursday's child has far to go.

[103] *Masahiro, is a Great Laughing-stock*
Sei with her usual sympathy for her fellow man seems to enjoy regaling us with the Groucho-like antics of this figure.

[104] *Things that are Distressing to See*
Sei takes objection to seeing unattractive people rising from a midday nap, their faces bloated with sleep and making a display of their slovenliness. I hate to see homeless people sitting on the pavement on a winter's day.

[105] *Things that are Hard to Say*
Today the students were talking after a long break. They seemed highly strung, more than they usually were. They were gossiping about their drinking habits...the word paralytic was mentioned.

[106] *Barrier Gates*

In Belfast, we still have 88 peace walls. This is one in Cupar Street: this wall divides the Falls and the Shankill. The gates are mostly situated in interface areas.

[107] *Forests*
My favourite forest is the one outside Portglenone.

[108] *Plains*
Ireland's central plain is located in the Shannon basin. Its limestone base is covered with layers of glacial drift, which is thick in the east but thin in the west.

[109] *Around the End of the Fourth Month*
I have been on a pilgrimage to Lough Derg. This is an excerpt from my novel *Lough Derg Tales:*

If you were heading to Lough Derg, the coach stopped there so that the pilgrims could have a last break before getting the boat over to the island. The boat left every day over the summer between 11am and 3pm. As David rattled through the towns, he recalled his father telling him that if you looked back when leaving the island, you would return for sure. He also remembered him saying, "there was a choppy sea once and everyone in the boat drowned" and remembered asking if it was on the way out to the island, or was it on the way back. He recalled his father laughing and saying, "What strange questions you ask son!" But he remembered thinking it was not a bit strange. For if it was on the way back, surely you would have had more time to prepare, so to speak, before meeting God. His father was not so concerned with these spiritual quandaries. He used to tell him stories about Lough Derg and how it came about. "Saint Patrick established it," father would say with certainty, "that's why it's called "St Patrick's Purgatory."

A few years ago, I also went to Lourdes. It was a wonderful trip. I bathed in the healing waters. It was a surreal experience. After queuing up for some time, you put on a robe and two people escort you to a bath and you are lowered into the water. It was like a death experience. Maybe that is how I will feel when I am dying.

The place was thronging with people from all over the world. It was my first visit to the France. I practised my French when making purchases. I hear some people complain that it has become too commercialised, with all its shops selling Lourdes medals, apparition statues, ornaments and rosary beads.

[110] *Common Things that Suddenly Sound Special*
In Zen the ordinary everyday mind is the way. Charlotte Beck wrote *Nothing Special: Everyday Zen* where she stresses the importance of forsaking our daydreams and accepting the present moment. Jōshu asked Nansen, "What is the way?" Nansen said "ordinary mind is the way."

[111] *Things That Lose by Being Painted*
Rilke wrote, 'Painting is something that takes place among the colours. And one has to leave them alone completely so that

they can settle the matter among themselves. Their intercourse: this is the whole of painting. Whoever arranges, meddles, injects his human deliberation, his wit, his advocacy, his intellectual agility, in any way is already disturbing and clouding their activity.'

I took this picture of a cherry tree in Benburb Priory gardens.

[112] *Things That Gain by Being Painted*
Today I went to the Andy Warhol exhibition in the MAC arts venue in Cathedral Quarter, Belfast. There were the iconic images of Marilyn Munroe and Elizabeth Taylor, Dollar Sign and Hamburger and pop art wallpaper featuring Mao. He said that everyone has fifteen minutes of fame. I also saw his amazing floating silver pillows. It was stunning. I just stood in the annex room and looked up at them floating up to the ceiling. He said art was how much you can get away with.

[113] *Winter is Best When it's Fearfully Cold*
This was not the worst winter but there have been some terribly cold days over the past few months. My home has high ceilings and it is hard to heat so I cannot agree with Sei's sentiments.

[114] *Moving Things*
Sei starts this entry with the profoundly moving image of a child dressed in mourning for a deceased parent. Funerals are deeply moving. I attended a funeral today in St Patrick's Church, Donegall Street. As I approached the church I noticed the funeral hearse. The priest commended the dead woman for her faith and devotion to the sacraments.

[115] *It's Delightful to be on Retreat*

Going on retreat was obviously a joy for Sei, although as always she condemns the behaviour of the commoners who push forward to get a glimpse of the sacred images. Every December, I go an interfaith retreat to Benburb Priory, which is led by Robert Kennedy, S.J., Roshi. He flies over from New York to lead the retreat. It is usually freezing cold and the roads to the Priory are narrow and winding after you leave Moy village. The retreat/sesshin is usually close to the winter solstice, so that is a special time as well. There is a passage grave monument at Newgrange, in the Boyne valley, where the chamber floor is illuminated by a shaft of sunlight from the rising sun and this occurs exactly on the solstice. I read some beautiful Waka poetry this morning in the Zen Centre. These come from *Moon in a Dewdrop*:

Waka,
On Non-dependence of Mind

Water birds
going and coming
their traces disappear
but they never
forget their path

Bowing Formally

A snowy heron
on the snowfield
where winter grass is
    unseen
hides itself
in its own figure

I took this picture of an eagle which I saw in St. Anne's Cathedral. It's amazing how the West adopts the image of an eagle to evoke spirituality whereas the East prefers the 'snowy heron'.

I also read from Dogen's Birth and Death/Shoji:

Because a Buddha is in birth and death, there is no birth and death.

Dogen's teachings on life and death are insightful. He says, 'if life comes there is life, if death comes, there is death. There is no need to be under their control.'

[116] *Deeply Irritating Things*

Sei chastises men for heading off to the Kamo festival, and not asking one of the young women to accompany them. She considers their behaviour crass.

I find it irritating when people change dates of events at short notice. This happened recently and I was annoyed. I hate when people lose the invoices and paperwork I have sent them and then I do not get paid. I am still waiting to be paid for work I did in December.

[117] *Miserable-looking Things*

Sei displays a lack of sympathy for a traveller in a drab place, riding in a dowdy carriage, being pulled by a dowdy ox. She cannot abide the sight of an aged beggar. I never could describe anything as looking miserable. I tend to be an optimist. When I had the 'flu last week I felt really miserable. Recently I went to see a film, *Les Miserables*. It was a wonderful film. The hero, Jean Valjean had been sent to prison for stealing a loaf of bread. When he gets out, he is pursued by Inspector Javert.

[118] *Things that Look Stiflingly Hot*
In this country it is rarely Stiflingly Hot. However if it is a hot summer's day, and I am driving, it can become extremely hot. If I park the car and then return to it, the steering wheel can feel like a hot poker.

[119] *Embarrassing Things*
Crude remarks embarrass me. I used to worry about the home I grew up in because it was not well decorated. I visited my friend's house in Coleraine and I was amazed at her kitchen and bathroom. She had her own room. I shared a bedroom with five sisters when I was growing up.

[120] *Awkward and Pointless Things*
Sometimes I spend a whole morning carrying out internet searches and then I feel I have wasted time. It's like an addiction.

[121] *Prayers and Incantations*
This is Lent and I have been meditating on the Passion of Christ. My prayer life is my mainstay. I have been reading a book on Thomas Merton. I am similar to him in that I love spiritual poetry. For example I think G.M. Hopkins was one of the greatest English poets. He wrote a wonderful sonnet called 'The Windhover':
I caught this morning's minion dauphin dapple dawn drawn Falcon, in
His riding of the rolling level underneath him steady air.

[122] *Awkward and Embarrassing Things*
It is not pleasant to hear someone back-biting about you. I used to work in an office in a local health trust and everyone seemed to spend their time gossiping and backbiting. It was a toxic place. I left it in 1999. After my second interview for the new job I had applied for, I walked into the city centre just as a

lunar eclipse was taking place. I just knew my life was going to change for ever.

[123] *The Regent was to Emerge from the Black Door*
Royal visits seemed to co-exist with days of abstinence, causing Her Majesty to remark, 'it seems to me that one would do far better to become a Buddha than a regent.'

[124] *It is Beautiful the Way the Water Drops Hang so Thick*
It is wonderful to see raindrops dripping off roses. I have a camellia in my garden and it is almost miraculous how it blooms every spring.

[125] *When we Gathered the Herbs*
This entry highlights the way Japanese people honour nature. At this Festival of Young Herbs, Sei longs to recite a poem which would reflect on the children's charming efforts to name one of the plants.

[126] *In the Second Month an Event Called the Selection*
Sei states her ignorance of what event is actually taking place but she does not hesitate in discussing the protocols around a flirtatious message from The Master of the Household. The elegance surrounding the latter's presentation of heitan cakes, strikes one as being archaic but nonetheless very charming.

[127] *One Day someone Idly Said*
Sei reflects on the strange names of garments. Over this winter I noticed some children wearing spirit hoods, which I think is a great name. They are a hat and scarf combination and are made of acrylic fur. They can represent wolves, or bears.

[128] *After the Late Regent's Death*

The tradition of honouring the dead is a central tenet of Buddhist practices. In this excerpt Captain Tadanobu, recites a Chinese poem for Her Majesty who is in mourning:

> Once more the moon comes round to autumn
> But where is he gone who loved it then.

In the Catholic faith, there is the tradition of having a 'month's mind' which is a special mass said for the deceased one month after he/she has died. I think it is a great idea. It is nice for the deceased's family to get together again. It is another chance to show respect for the dead.

[129] *One Evening, Secretary Controller Yukinari*

Sei once again demonstrates her poetic virtuosity. Recently I went to the Seamus Heaney writing group. One of the poems was based on John O'Donohue's book, *To Bless the Space Between Us: A Book of Blessings:*

> 'For Death'
> From the moment you were born
> Your death has walked beside you
> Though it seldom shows its face,
> You still feel its empty touch
> When fear invades your life,
> Or what you love is lost
> Or inner damage is incurred…

Paul, one of member's of the group wrote this version:

> From the moment you were born
> Your death has walked beside you

Without showing its face.
When fear invades your life

Or what you love is lost
You feel death's empty touch
Deep in your heart.

[130] *One Dark Moonless Night*
This excerpt demonstrates Sei's sharp's mind when she responds to an incident with a clever poem.

[131] *When the Year of Mourning*
This entry shows the kind of practical jokes that were part of court life. The message to Emperor Ichijo's nurse Tosanmi implies that a lack of respect has been shown in respect of mourning attire for the late emperor.

It also reminds me of the scene in *Gone With the Wind* where Scarlet O'Hara is criticised by her society for coming out of her widow's weeds too soon.

[132] *Occasions When the Time Drags by*
Everybody hates a rainy day and as a denizen of Ireland, I have witnessed many wet days. Tonight I am teaching Social Policy. When I worked in the Health Service I heard these terms, community care and purchaser/provider split. I read about Barbara Robb's experience of her treatment in Ely, a long-term stay hospital for those suffering from mental health problems. Her book, *Sans Everything* documented her experiences and she campaigned to have this type of long-term hospital closed. However not all long-term institutions were bad. *The Observer* newspaper praised Graylingwell Hospital in the following glowing terms:

Patients have every convenience at hand for night requirements, even down to carpet slippers. Blinds and curtains give a home-like comfort to the windows. Books, papers and magazines are liberally provided, while dominoes, cards and games of many kinds serve to cheer and lighten the evenings.

[133] *Things that Relieve such Occasions*
At the moment I am getting inspiration from Dogen's teaching. He wrote, 'Water does not flow but the bridge flows.' He also explained these two words from the Sandokai, or Harmony of Difference or Same:

Mei and An,

In the light there is darkness,
but don't take it as darkness.
In the dark there is light,
but don't see it as light.
Meichu ni atatte an ari

[134] *Worthless Things*
Society tends to value money and status. I am more interested in the ordinary, the commonplace.

Sei makes the comment that she never intended her book to be seen by others so she felt she should write down whatever popped into her and never worried how she would be judged. I once read that we all write with an audience in mind. It may a subconscious desire to connect.

[135] *Things that are Truly Splendid*
I took this photograph of a cobweb in the bushes outside Maryville Tea Rooms on the Lisburn Road.

Frozen primroses in Union Street as I walked from the train to the college. I wrote this poem after reading *Wild Flowers by* John Gilmour and Max Walters, which was in the college library.

Wild Flowers

Mountain habitat
Snowdon, 1950

Wood Sorrell in April
Winter Aconite in February
Wood Anemone in April
Common Violet in April
Sedge on a woodland
    glade

Lady's mantle
Wild Angelica
Sea pink
Green spleenwort
Harebell
Ox-eye daisy
Mountain sorrel
Mossy saxifrage
Purple saxifrage
Starry saxifrage
Alpine saw-wort
Rose-root
Miss campion
Devil's bit scabious

[136] *After the Regent had Departed this Life*
Sei's entry describes the way she had become a target for
malicious gossip after the death of the regent. She left court circles for a few months. This must have been a trying time for Sei.
As usual poetry played a part in her return when Her Majesty

sent her a message in a Kerria petal with the words, 'and never rises into words.' This world of rumour and Chinese whispers must have been tricky to negotiate.

[137] *It's Towards the Middle of the First Month*
Sei describes a scene where the children gather beneath the tree and ask a boy to cut some sticks for them to take back to their mistress who will use them for hare-mallets.

[138] *A Good-looking Man*
Sei describes an arrogant looking man who spends a whole day absorbed in a game of sugoroku.

[139] *It's Also Amusing to See*
Again Sei, always attuned to rank, describes the behaviour of a socially inferior man in a game of 'go'.

[140] *Alarming-looking Things*
Sei seems to find water chestnuts alarming! Again it hard to understand this aesthetic sensibility.

[141] *Things that Look Fresh and Pure*
Little girls making their first Holy Communion.
Giorgio Armani's Milan Collection/Garconne, womanly clothes with a gentlemanly edge. Black trousers with elongated darts under the pockets and ornamental zippers. Bib fronted trousers in black velvet and slouchy black hats based on Rastafarian headgear.

[142] *Distasteful-looking Things*
A man staggering down the road roaring and shouting. A woman shouting loudly at her child. Colours that clash.

[143] *Things that Make the Heart Lurch with Anxiety*
When I am studying a course I would get anxious if the coursework is not finished on time.

Being handed out a scenario in acting class. I used to dread it so much. I felt I had a break pedal on my creativity.

[144] *Endearingly Lovely Things*
New born lambs. One of my students showed me a picture of her Dorset lambs which she helped to birth.

Recently I showed a DVD called *Reflections on Elephants* which was produced by the National Geographic Society. Filmmakers, Ginger Mauney and her husband follow a herd of elephants in Ethosa Park, Africa. Knob Nose, the leader of the herd is driven by some irresistible unseen force and she seems to know when to drive the herd forward to a watering hole on a particular day. When the elephants reach the watering hole, they take a mud bath which puts a protective coating on their hide. She might suddenly stop and sniff the air, and then bring the herd to a halt. She knows which roads lead to water, which one to ruin as taking a wrong road can lead to oblivion. Another one of the matriarchs was called Doughnut, because she had a hole in her ear. Elephants communicate by sending infrasonic messages which are transmiited before sunrise or after sunset, as this improves the range due to temperature inversion. By eavesdropping on elephants you will be surprised to learn that they actually mourn over the loss of family members. In the elephant graveyard Knob Nose mourns for her two calves that have died. It almost seems as if she is whispering to the bones. She is so grief-stricken, she leaves the herd and wanders aimlessly for a few weeks. Just as we rarely hear about a Pope quitting, matriarchs rarely leave their herd. But in order to express the private language of her grief, Knob Nose felt she needed to mourn privately.

[145] *Times When Someone's Presence Produces Foolish Excitement*

I suppose it's easy to judge the way a mother controls or fails to control her child. Sometimes in the supermarket, a child will somehow detach herself from her mother and begin running up aisles, perhaps pulling a toy or packet of sweets from the shelves.

[146] *Things with Terrifying Names*

The name Frankenstein usually has the desired effect of frightening people. In *Frankenstein or The Modern Prometheus* by Mary Shelley, Victor Frankenstein created the monster, which was referred to as the 'monster' or the 'creature'.

On Saturday, my friend Irene and I went into Oxfam second hand shop on the Dublin Road. Irene bought *The Art of Sleep* by Sophie de Sivry and Philippe Meyer. I wrote this poem after returning from Tokyo:

I once saw a geisha girl when I was in Tokyo.
I saw a geisha girl
In downtown Tokyo
She was tripping along in zori
Wearing an elegant kimono
Tied with a obi

Her hair in a high chignon
Pinned up with a kanzashi
She was a free spirit
With a mobile phone
To her ear.

Eitaro is Japan's only male geisha who performs in the role as a female dancer. He is the master of an 'okiya,' a geisha house in Tokyo. We then went to the Ulster Museum, where there were art and pottery exhibitions. John Luke was known as Ulster's Craftsman Painter and John Hewitt as Ulster's Craftsman Poet. When he was young he worked in a Belfast Linen Mill and later in the shipyards. He attended the Belfast School of Art and then progressed on to the Slade School of Fine Art. In his craft he followed medieval and Renaissance techniques but at the same time his work engages with contemporary concerns.

Among the pottery and painting there was the following:

Rev H Dunbar's 'Porcelain Greyhounds'

'Porcelain Prince of Whales Ice Pails'

Gizela Sabokova's 'Glass pane" 1987
Jan Fisar, 'Cat and Dog', 1987
Shell cabaret set
Bittern comport, porcelain
Bute bowl and stand
Piggin
Pilgrimar,
Moon Flask

Sir Terry Frost's 'Mars Orange and Black'
William Scott's 'Shapes and Shadows'
Strickland Lowry's 'The family of Thomas Bateson of Orangefield', Co. Down.
George Barrett's' Sunrise and Ruins'
John Astley's, 'Sir Captain Molyneux, 3rd Baronet of Castle Dillon'
Eliz Magill's, 'Chronicles of Orange'
Derek Hill's 'Tory Island from Tor More'
Barrie Cooke's 'Big Tench Lake'

[147] *Things that Look Ordinary but Become Extraordinary when Written*

I agree with Sei's opinion that strawberry is a beautiful word. I found this little poem, a blazon or tribute to a woman:

ichot a burde in bower brigh
that sully semly is on sight
With locks lefliche and long
with frount and face fair to fond

The poem, 'Love for a Beautiful Lady' is from the late 13th century and I found it in Barry Spur's Studying *Poetry*. He also mentioned Judith Beveridge and Joanne Burns.

I saw frogspawn in the park today. It was like transparent tapioca with a little black ball bead in the middle. I think frogspawn is a beautiful word. These were the names of the newly baptised children in Holy Family Parish Bulletin:

February Baptisms

Ryan,
Briannagh,
Chuisle
Chloe
Cliona
Cadhla
Kaiden
Sophie

Steve Morris, a *Guardian* wildlife reporter wrote an article on the damage done to wildlife in 2012. I crafted a poem from the article:

I
Water voles'
holes and
Otter holts
Washed away
In torrents

Dormice had
A poor breeding
season
Animal sanctuaries
Beleaguered with underfed
Hedgehogs.
Badgers had a tough year
Bees, hoverflies and
Butterflies struggled.

Orchids prevailed

II
The bastard toadflex
and Grasshoppers
Need a few bare patches
In order to stay alive

Orchids triumphed

[148] *Repulsive Things*
I would find cockroaches repulsive.

[149] *Occasions When Something Inconsequential has its Day*
The bamboo breaking ceremonies, the presentation of hare-
mallets to the emperor evoke a quasi feudal world, tinged with
nostalgia.

[150] *People who Look as if Things are Difficult for Them*

A homeless person. A migrant whose English is poor and cannot find work.

CHAPTER FIVE:

Things now Useless that recall a Glorious Past

[151] *People who Seem Envious*
There is an expression, 'keeping up with the Joneses' where
you want as much money and status as your neighbour.

[152] *Things Whose Outcome you Long to Know*
I like the sound of these lines:
The various forms of tie-dyeing
Roll dye, apple dye.

[153] *Occasions for Anxious Waiting*
The result of the MOT test. When you car is four years old,
you have to take it to the Vehicle Test Centre in order to check
its roadworthiness. It's like bringing a child to school on his
first day. Once the tearful parent turns her back the new child
is led like a lamb and the new teacher will soon be putting him
to the test! When you drive in you have go to your allocated
lane and wait to be called. I never realised until a few years ago
that you were supposed to keep your engine running before
you are called in. The chap who waved me in on Saturday 9th
March 2013 was a cheery sort. There was some banter going
on with examiners in the other lanes. Computers were flashing,
the examiners were saying, 'switch on your dipped headlights,
your beam, your left and right indicator, fog light' and so forth.
Sometimes it is hard to make out if they are shouting at you or
drivers in the adjoining lanes. I usually mix up my lights and in-
dicators owning to stress and foreboding that the car might not

get through the test. Little blue lines went across the diagnostic monitor but I had no idea how to interpret the data. He pulled this little machine over to the headlights and then he asked me to adjust them. I had no idea what button this was, so the poor man had to locate it for me. It was sort of a dial thing that went from one to five. Have I been sending my headlights up to the sky, transmitting messages to Mars, or have I been blinding other drivers? I never drive with the full headlights on. My sister in Aghadowey says I should put on the beam when I am driving in the country. Sometimes those little country roads are dark and twisted. After the PC diagnostics, the examiner shoos you away like some kind of meddlesome hen and he drives the car up the yard. The driver has to sit behind a little cordoned off area and hang around there like a guilty man awaiting a verdict. Your car is suspended on high and an examiner scrutinises underneath looking for heaven knows what. I look on tremulously hoping the exhaust does not suddenly fall off. The man beside me has been summoned…looks like his estate car has got through. I am then called. A set of keys and an MOT Certificate dated until 10th March 2014 is like I have received a reprieve from a jail sentence.

[154] *When the Empress was in Mourning for the Previous Regent*

It's Sunday 10th March 2013 and I noticed a funeral cortège heading towards St Patrick's Church, Donegall Street. The coffin was being carried. I noticed the hearse had a display which spelled out the words NANA. I think that was what it spelled out. The mourners were walking in a dignified manner. It was almost dusk and I could see the beguiling stain glass windows in the church. I suddenly remembered that this was Mother's Day. In Buddhism you do not let the prospect of death scare you. In the early days the novices were sent off to meditate in charnel grounds.

An air of whimsy pervades this long entry where Sei refers to herself as the connoisseur of whimsy. Her capricious flirtations with Tadanobu and their secret language make them an intriguing couple. They use the language of go as a secret code to describe courtship. Modern language is permeated with *double entendre* and it can become tedious after a while.

This interchange with Nobukatu is rather nasty. The atmosphere in the court ranged from interludes of poetry and religious observance to downright cattiness. The internet has provided humanity with infinite number of sites and platforms to be spiteful. I read in the *Belfast Telegraph* today (11/12/13) that a Belfast schoolgirl, Shaneice Nesbitt who was invited to a private party by *One Direction's* Harry Styles after the show. After news got out via Twitter and Facebook she was inundated with messages and questions. She even received a death threat.

Maybe Styles's actions compromised this girl's safety. Just because he is rich has he the right to send bodyguards over to her to ask for her number? Should a schoolgirl be partying in the Culloden Hotel to 4am with a high profile pop star...whose treatment of former girlfriends is hardly honourable.

[155] *The Name Kokiden Referred to the High Consort*
It was unpleasant for Sei to live in such highly charged atmosphere of intrigue and innuendo.

[156] *Things now Useless that recall a Glorious Past*
A mother who has once been the mainstay of the family but now has to go into a nursing home because no one is either able to or willing to care for her.

[157] *Situation you have a Feeling will Turn out Badly*
My aunt will 95 on the 1st April. She shares the same date of birth as my late father. When I was at St John's Primary School in Swatragh, the headmaster asked one day 'if you were born on

the same date as someone, would you be the same age?' I was the only one who knew the correct answer. One day he asked, 'which was heavier: a pound of lead or a pound of feathers?'

'Close the window of the light/And it will be all right' was playing on the radio at lunch time.

Big grey clouds amble across the sky making patterns. Now it looks like a map of Europe with with a soldier hovering over it, now it is like a cross between Don Quixote and a samurai warrior.

[158] *Sutra Reading*
For the past fifteen years, I have been chanting the Metta Sutta. The chant comes from the Tripitaka, or the Sutta Nipata, which is from the Sutrs-pitaka, or Sutra Basket.

Metta is a Pali word meaning compassion, or a benevolence towards all sentient beings. By reciting this sutta I am supposed to become free of attachments and great desire. One of the lines is, 'let us not desire great possession even for ourselves or our family, let us not be submerged by the things of the world, let us not take upon ourselves the burden of riches.'

[159] *Things that are Near Yet Far*
You might have grown up in the same house as your siblings and yet when you have grown up and grown apart, you might never see them.

[160] *Things that are Far Yet Near*
Once at a Zen talk given by Robert Kennedy, he said there's only a hair's breadth between heaven and earth. Case 17, Hogen's Hair's-Breadth, from *The Book of Equanimity* states that, 'If there's even a hair's breadth of difference, heaven and earth are clearly separated.' Shuzan replied, 'if there's even a hair's breadth of difference, heaven and earth are clearly separated.'

To me this means that if we are attached to our agendas we will suffer. Gerry Wick said that 'we walk around with big hooks sticking out of our bodies. Anyone can come by, jerk them and upset us.'

While researching Hogens' Hair's-Breadth I came across the Shinjinmei/faith mind poem of Master Sozan.

[161] *Wells*

I made a pilgrimage to Cooey's Well last month. It is situated outside Portaferry. It is one of the most peaceful places I have ever visited in my life. I always come away renewed.

[162] *Plains*

Entry 13, deals with plains. The plains that Sei mentions would all have[11] been linked to famous poems. I like this poem of Antaine Ó Raifteir, (1784–1835):

Anois teacht an Earraigh
beidh an lá dúl chun shíneadh,
Is tar eis na féil Bríde
ardóigh mé mo sheol.
Go Coillte Mach rachad
ní stopfaidh me choíche
Go seasfaidh mé síos
i lár Chondae Mhaigh Eo.

I gClár Chlainne Mhuiris
A bheas mé an chéad oíche,
Is I mballa taobh thíos de
A thosós mé ag ól
Go Coillte Mách rachad
Go ndéanfad cuairt mhíosa ann
I bhfogas dhá mhíle
Do Bhéal an átha Mhóir.

Fágaim le huacht é
go n-éiríonn mo chroí-se
Mar a éiríonn an ghaoth
nó mar a scaipeann an ceo
Nuair a smaoiním ar Cheara
nó ar Ghaileang taobh thíos de
Ar Sceathach an Mhíle
nó ar phlánaí Mhaigh Eo.

This is Frank O'Connor's translation:

Now with the springtime
The days will grow longer
And after St Bride's day'
My sail I'll let go
I put my mind to it,
And I never will linger
Till I find myself back
In the County Mayo.
In Clare of Morris family
I will be the first night
and in the Wall on the side below it
I will begin to drink
to Maghs Woods I shall go
until I shall make a months visit there
two miles close
to the Mouth of the Big Ford.

I swear
that my heart rises up
as the wind rises up
or as the fog lifts
when I think about Ceara
or about Gaileang on the lower side of it

about Sceathach an Mhíle
or about the plains of Mayo.

[163] *Court Nobles*
There is a system of hereditary peerage in the Britain but
this notion has been challenged.

[164] *Nobles*
In *Antony and Cleopatra,* the former states, the 'nobleness of
life is to do thus.'

[165] *Acting Provisional Governors*
Once I worked in an office and if someone had left and
no replacement had been found, a person in the grade below
would have been asked to 'act up'.

[166] *Commissioners*
The Lords Commissioners are privy councillors who carry
out certain functions such as the opening and prorogation of
Parliament, or the granting of royal assent.

[167] *Priests*
There was a very old parish priest in our church when I was
young. He used to genuflect every time he walked past the altar
and he would recite, 'blessed be Jesus in the most holy sacrament of the altar.'

[168] *Ladies*
We have no royal family in Northern Ireland. However le-
gally we are part of the UK, although we have a devolved gov-
ernment. The Queen lives in Buckingham Palace in London.
On 17/03/13 a programme, *'Our Queen'*, focused on Queen
Elizabeth II's diamond jubilee celebrations. In the programme,
the highlights of her golden year were shown, from the flotilla

on the Thames to the street parties. It takes a huge staff to look after the palace. If you want to work there you are required to do a diploma for footmen and butlers. One of the jobs is to stamp the crown on the butter. The Queen's dresses, have to be bright but not ornate. The programme showed the Queen inspecting the banqueting table. She asked the butlers to move the fruit bowls a little back. There are six glasses for every guest. The Queen prefers unobtrusive microphones. The florists produced amazing displays. There was a Halloween theme with lots of orange, pumpkin coloured flowers.

[169] *Sixth-rank Chamberlains*
In the British monarchy, the Lord Chamberlain is the senior official of the Royal Household. He is responsible for organising court events and state dinners.

[170] *A Place Where a Lady Lives Alone*
I remember when we all went to school my grandmother was left alone in the house all day. She was a saint.

[171] *The Home of a Lady in Court Service*
The mores of courtship must have been so convoluted in such highly sophisticated court circles.

Sei recounts an archetypal tale of romance where a certain gentleman visits a Lady Someone. Today these stories are recounted in Mills & Boon books.

[172] *One Day in the Ninth Month*
Sei's next entry is written in the same tone as the previous entry.

[173] *It is Quite Delightful When the Snow is Falling*
We have had an unseasonal fall of snow. Temperatures dropped rapidly and we woke up to a winter wonderland on Friday 22nd March 2013. This is an image of Cave Hill.

This a poem is I wrote in response to the snow:

Lambs

Farmer McCrory's
Lambs buried in six feet of
  snow

We don't understand
Last year we were sheltering
Under trees for shade
Now we are shivering
Under six feet of snow
Our lambs are coming
Our lambs are freezing
Our lambs are dying

After two days farmers'
hands are pulling
Us rudely from the
Cold white tomb
By the horns and
We are thrown like
Widows on a pyre
Kindly midwife
Now turned
Rough rescuer

Now we're huddling
In the corner of
A field.

The gritters are out
Some people's lights are out
The emergency services are out

Schools are closed
Offices are shut
Cars have crashed

Wendy Austin says it is not nice snow
Horseradishes are hard to get out of the ground.
It hurts your face

[174] *Once During the Reign of the Former Emperor Murakami*
Snow, moonlight and blossoms...pure poetry.

[175] *The Lady Known as Miare no Seji*
This lady presented the emperor with a beautifully crafted handmade doll.

Great attention was paid to the arts during the Heian period, 797-1180. Before coming into contact with the Chinese, Japanese was an oral language. After borrowing the kangi characters from the Chinese, the written script was only used for official documents. During this period, court nobles adapted the script to produce poetry and calligraphy. This was finessed even further and an emphasis was placed on the type of paper used, and quite often a sprig or herb was sent along with the letter, thereby producing a highly coded message. Behind the screens and sophistication of this highly stylised court, an aesthetic emerged which communicated the daily conspiracies and interactions at the Imperial Palace. To participate in this sophisticated coterie you needed to be highly educated and have quick wits.

The word 'heian' means tranquillity or peace and this period is now considered one of the most illustrious times in Japanese history. Some of their activities might strike us as frivolous today and some could say elitist. Sei's comments are a far cry from being politically correct. The court consisted of a few high-ranking noble families who were greedy for power and control. The Fujiwari clan was one of the most prominent families. There was a clear demarcation between the court and the commoners.

[176] *When I First Went into Court Service*
This reminds of my first day at school. I felt like a trapped animal. Would I have to be quiet from now on? The prospect appalled me. I was crushed like a clove of garlic.

[177] *People who Feel Smug*
I was teaching the differences between positivists and phenomenologists this afternoon. The positivists feel smug with their scientific approach whereas phenomenologists focus on actual phenomena, what we actually see, hear, touch, taste and feel.

[178] *Nothing is More Splendid Than Rank*
The new Pope, Francis I, seems to disdain the trappings of rank. He said, 'the Pope must open his arms to protect all of God's people and embrace with tender affection the whole of humanity, especially the poorest, the weakest and the least important.' Michael Day commented that things never go according to plan for he was soon shaking hands with heads of state,

including Mugabe, Baroness Warsi, the Duke of Gloucester and Ken Clarke. He took a tour in his open-topped Popemobile, criss-crossing the piazza, stopping to bless a disabled man, shaking hands and kissing babies.

[179] *Awe Inspiring Things*
It's the spring equinox 2013 and the cherry trees are coming into bloom. I noticed two beautiful ones as I drove down Fortwilliam Park as I was heading to Ballymena to teach.

[180] *Illnesses*
My sister contracted Bell's palsy this year. She then found out that in fact she had shingles and she is taking a lot of medication. She has been off work for two months.

[181] *It is Delightful to See One Who is a Great Ladies' Man*
A ladies' man these days would be a man who seeks out and enjoys female company. He would not be as predatory as a Casanova or a seducer. Mary Pohl wrote an article entitled, 'James Bond: the Biggest Ladies' Man of Them All.' In the article she argues that Bond is incapable of sustaining a relationship. In the Bond movie, *On Her Majesty's Secret Service*, (1969), the Bond hero, George Lazenby marries Contessa di Vicenzo, but she gets killed. In *Casino Royale*, (2006), Daniel Craig's love interest, Vesper Lynd, is also killed.

[182] *It's the Middle of a Fiercely Hot Day*
I have just returned from Carrickfergus, and it was freezing cold. However yesterday my neighbour Annette and her son Darragh presented me with beautiful Easter gifts. There was a beautiful bunch of narcissi, a Cadbury's Mini Eggs chocolate gateau, and a box of Cadbury's Mini Eggs chocolate nest eggs. The gifts were in a pink polka dot gift bag. There was also a card with an Easter image of a cute little rabbit, a little yellow

chick standing beside a cracked white shell surrounded by lots of primroses. The message read 'with lots of love.'

[183] *The Floorboards of the Southern or Perhaps the Eastern Aisle*
I prefer floorboards to carpet.

[184] *It is Enchanting to Overhear*
The other day I heard a woman tell a child, 'I don't need passwords. I have nothing to hide'.

[185] *Things That Prove Disillusioning*
A woman who lost livestock in the recent snowstorm talked about her distress at the death of her ewes, which she called 'yows'.

[186] *It's Very Unseemly For a Man*
I heard an expression at work that, 'manners maketh the man'.

[187] *Winds*
There was a bitter east wind today and I wrapped up well as I walked around the Waterworks Park today. There was a Bird Club meeting and I stopped to find out more about it. Aidan had netted a male and female blackbird and was ringing them.

[188] *The Day after a Typhoon*
We had an avalanche on Sunday 24/03/13. I thought the roof was coming down. I took a photograph of the damage caused to the guttering:

[189] *Elegantly Intriguing Things*
Ballet dancers and swans.

[190] *Islands*

Harry Clifton argues that Irish people are a desperate people who, 'could make a god out of anything. Black kelp/For the fields, a bullock washed ashore/That fed us for months, without His Majesty's help.' He also wrote that we are a pitiful people:

> People, you see, without a nation,
> Only a gut metaphysics
> Bilge-pumped to infinity
> On a leaking vessel
>
> Fleeing westward, Irish Greeks,
> For whom the word sea
> Meant nothing, who could only speak
> Of blind force, necessity.

[191] *Beaches*
My favourite beaches are in Portstewart, Portrush and Cushendall. I once walked along a beach in Cannes and it was beautiful. I was there visiting my sister who has an apartment in Nice.

[192] *Bays*
Last summer I volunteered at the Peace Camp installation at Whitepark Bay. It was an extraordinary experience. Instead of staring at my computer screen and googling everything under the sun, I was able to look out at the endless horizon and

imagine sea myths, sea creatures and even mermaids. I saw a little fishing boat and a man fishing in the middle of the grey billowy sea. Sea birds dipped into the water looking for fish. Maybe the birds were fulmars, which patrol the coastline in this area. Ringed plovers, white throats and meadow pipits are also commonly seen birds on the North Antrim coast. I saw a herd of cows at the top of the beach. Such a change from my usual inner city landscape in Belfast.

The Peace Camp is part of the London 2012 Festival. This is a nationwide show and camps will appear in Cuckmere Haven, Seven Sisters, East Sussex, Cemaes Bay, Anglesey, Wales, Downhill Beach/Mussenden Temple, Whitepark Bay, Ford Fiddes, and Cliff Beach (Isle of Lewis) in Scotland, Dunstanburgh Castle, England and Godfrey, England. The Peace Camp event was produced by Artichoke Trust as part of the Cultural Olympiad and London 2012 Festival. The events are funded by the Arts Council, England, Legacy Trust UK and the Olympic Lottery Distributor. The Artichoke Trust is responsible for producing large-scale spectacular events. The idea of the peace camp was inspired by the tradition of calling a truce during the Olympic Games, so that the competitors could participate in a safe environment. Also in ancient Greece, there were poetry and philosophy competitions running at the same time as the sports.

The encampments in Whitepark Bay and Downhill Beach/ Mussenden Temple are part one of Northern Ireland's Our Time, Our Place campaign. Deborah Warner, one of the UK's most important theatre directors whose recent site-specific installations include *The St Pancras Project* and *The Tower Project,* London, created the Peace Camp in collaboration with Fiona Shaw, whose stage credits included *London Assurance, Mother Courage* and *Richard II* at the

National Theatre. The soundscape was created by Mel Mercier and John Del'Nero.

It was an extraordinary experience.

[193] *Woods*

When I hear the word 'woods', I always think of Robert Frost's famous poem, 'Stopping by Woods on a Snowy Evening'. I think it is one of the most perfect poems in the world.

Terri Windling commented that 'the fairy tale journey may look like an outward trek across plains and mountains, through castles and forests, but the actual movement is inwards, into the lands of the soul. The dark path of the fairy tale forest lies in the shadow of our imagination, the depths of our unconscious. To travel to the wood, to face its dangers, is to emerge transformed by this experience.'

[194] *Temples*

Mount Stewart, ancestral home of the Marquis of Londonderry has exquisite gardens and a wonderful octagonal building called The Temple of Winds.

[195] *Sutras*

The sutra spoken by the Sixth Patriarchs on the High Seat of the Treasure of the Law is, according to Heinrich Dumoulin, the only Zen text that can be called 'Sutra'. Hui-neng, a poor wood-cutter, became one of Sixth Patriarch of the Dhyana School. Hung-gen, the master of Wang-mei monastery set his disciples the task of composing a poem which manifested their enlightenment. Shen-hsiu wrote:

The body is the Bodhi tree (enlightenment),
The mind is a clear mirror standing.
Take care to wipe it all the time,
Allow no grain of dust to cling.

Hui-neng composed the following:
The Bodhi is not like a tree,
The clear mirror is nowhere standing.
Fundamentally not one thing exists;
Where, then, is a grain of dust to cling?

[196] *Buddhas*

Today, 3rd April 2013 I am on holidays. No teaching until 8th April. I have just been reading Zen Master Seung Sahn's *The Compass of Zen*. He explains The Eight Sufferings:

Birth, old age, sickness, death, being separated from those you love, being in the presence of those you dislike, not getting what you desire, the imbalance of the five skandas. The Buddha said that we do not have a self, but rather our mind is a 'fleeting combination of changing energies, divided in five aggregates: forms, feelings, perceptions, impulses and consciousness.' (Sahn, 61) When these aggregates or skandas are out of balance, great suffering results. Sahn uses the example of an obese person, whose tongue says give me more sweets, but whose body wants to practise moderation.

[197] *Chinese Writings*

Sei mentions Bo Juyi, a prominent Chinese poet (772-846) whose poems reflected everyday concerns. His poetic style became known as Yuan-Bai-Ti, or Fundamentally Plain Form, and he also invented a poetry framework known as 'Yu Yuan Jiu Shu' or 'Nine Principles of Poetry.'

Remembering South of the River
South of the river is good,
Long ago, I knew the landscape well.
At sunrise the flowers are red like fire,
In spring, the river's water's green as lilies.
How could I not remember south of the river?

[198] *Tales*

I enjoy reading folk and fairytales. Recently I have been to see an updated version of '*Hansel and Gretel*' and '*Jack and the Beanstalk*'. Under the Aarne-Thompson classification, *Hansel and Gretel* is classed under Class 327. The tale is of German origin and was recorded by the Brothers Grimm. Hansel and Gretel are two young children, who are abandoned in the forest and fall into the hands of a wicked witch who lives in a house made of cake and confectionary. The clever boy and girl outwit the cannibalistic witch and return home in triumph.

Jack and the Beanstalk is from the English fairy tale tradition. It is similar to *Jack the Giant Killer*. Benjamin Tabart produced the story in 1807. Another version was written by Henry Cole in 1842. Joseph Jacob's version appeared in *The English Fairy Tales,* 1809. In the tale a young boy is sent to the market to sell a cow but instead of bringing the money back to his impoverished mother he brings back magic beans which he accepted as payment. Jack is sent to bed without supper and his mother throws the beans out. The next day a huge beanstalk has grown which Jack climbs. He has an amazing adventure and by fairy magic he is able to outwit the giant by stealing his gold, his golden egg laying hen and his magic harp. The famous refrain in the tale is universally known and loved:

Fee-Fi-Fo-Fum
I smell the blood of an Englishman

Be he alive, or be he dead
I grind his bones for my bread.

[199] *Darani Incantations*

A Darani or dharani comes from the Sanskrit word meaning to maintain or hold. A Darani is akind of incantation which may be used to invoke a particular blessing or protection. In the chant book we use in the Zen Centre, there is a darini called Kan Ro Mon which is a chant for summoning deceased spirits to the great assembly. There is also one for blessing food with the unimpeded radiance of innumerable virtues and one for completely banishing fear, freeing all from rebirths as hungry ghosts.

[200] *Musical Performances*

I heard that the musical *Cats* and the film musical *Mama Mia* have been translated into Mandarin and are now being performed and shown in China.

CHAPTER SIX:

Things That No one Notices

[201] *Games*

I am just after speaking to my nephew Jake and his friend Teddy in Gotto's sports shop in Stranmillis. They had been playing cricket all morning. Teddy said that they beat the second year students. I think I probably asked a silly question which was 'what position did you play?' The look of incredulity I received from them both made me realise I had committed a *faux pas*. My sister informed me that it's about scores. I looked it up on the internet and it said that there are two batsmen, one at each wicket and one bowler. The bowler bowls the ball and as far as I can gather the batsmen runs up and down between the wickets...there are some other rules but at the end when there is only one batsman left out of the team of eleven he has no partner and is referred to as 'not out', and that means the innings for that side is over. I will now write down all my entire cricket vocabulary:

- Innings: I have heard the expression, 'he/she had a good innings'.
- Crease
- Runs
- Maiden over
- Fieldsman
- Umpire

The Olympic Games, which ran from 27th July to 12th August, were hosted by Britain this year. As I was busy with amateur dramatics at this time, I can honestly say I saw none of the games. I had this idea that I would write an article on not watching the games, but somehow hearing about the highlights on the radio. I can remember standing in my kitchen in Kansas Avenue in north Belfast and seeing a streak of red in the sky as the Red Arrows flew across at 1pm to herald the start of the games on 27th July, 2012. It was great to feel I was a part of something bigger. I then recall a lot of hype about the opening and Danny Boyle's name was everyone's lips, the Queen jumped out a helicopter, and had met Mr Bond and then there was something about nurses jumping on hospital beds and something about sheep to represent this green and pleasant land. Bradley Wiggins won a medal and there was someone called Mo Farah who was staring out from a billboard on the Shore Road at the bottom of Fortwilliam.

[202] *Dances*

I loved going to dances when I was a teenager. Our local dance hall was the Marian Hall in Kilrea. There was no alcohol, a priest kept eye on proceedings as it was a parish dance and if you 'went out with a boy' you got left home to your house.

[203] *Plucked Instruments*

I love the sound of the violin. In Shakespeare's *Much Ado About Nothing*, Benedick remarks, 'Is it not strange that sheep's guts should hale souls out of men's bodies?' Neuroscientists are now studying the way music affects our mood. Apparently, music stimulates the release of dopamine from the dorsal and ventral striatum. A trumpet indicated the approach of royalty whereas the lute signified more carnal interests as these words from Richard III testify:

And now,--instead of mounting barbed steeds
To fright the souls of fearful adversaries,--

He capers nimbly in a lady's chamber
To the lascivious pleasing of a lute.

[204] *Wind Instruments*
One of my favourite pieces of music is 'Stranger on the Shore'
a clarinet piece written by Acker Bilk for his daughter:

Here I stand, watching the
    tide go out
So all alone and blue
Just dreaming dreams of
    you

I watched your ship as it
    sailed out to sea
Taking all my dreams
And taking all of me

*I took this photograph in
Warrenpoint in January 2013*

The sighing of the waves
The wailing of the wind
The tears in my eyes burn
Pleading, "My love, return"

Why, oh, why must I go on like this?
Shall I just be a lonely stranger on the shore?

[205] *Spectacles*
'White clouds in the wind
are parted by the mountain
peak and seen no more...as
your cold heart at parting/
holds no traces of regret' by
Mibu no Tadamine is a nostalgic Japanese poem.

[206] *Around the Fifth Month*
This passage reminds me of the reeds growing on the upper lake of the Waterworks which is always beautiful to witness.

[207] *When it's Fearfully Hot*
It's the 17/04/13 and it has been wet and windy the past few days but at least the temperatures are starting to rise.

[208] *On the Evening of the Fourth Day of the Fifth Month*
I am in Newtownabbey College now and I have been listening to Margaret Thatcher's funeral in St Paul's Cathedral. Big Ben was silenced and roads were closed off…people looked on from offices windows trying to get a glimpse. There was immaculate WWI gun carriage which had been polished for the occasion. The coffin was placed on the gun carriage and taken to St. Paul's Cathedral. Sei would have approved of the pomp and ceremony displayed throughout. And I am glad to hear the horses will get a special treat of apples and carrots when they get home.

[209] *On the Way to the Kamo Shrine*
In this funny excerpt, Sei complains about the mocking song they sing about the cuckoo.

[210] *At the End of the Eighth Month*
I will be going on retreat to Benburb Priory from 23rd to 28th August.

[211] *Soon After the End of the Eight Month*
I remember when I did a sesshin in SFZC, I had to get up early and followed a demanding schedule.

[212] *Setting off to Climb the Slope*
Croagh Patrick is the holiest mountain in Ireland. It overlooks Clew Bay in County Mayo. Every year on the last Sunday

of July, thousands of pilgrims climb the 764-metre mountain in their bare feet. The slope has many stones and loose shale. The climb is done in honour of St Patrick, the patron saint of Ireland.

[213] *The Sweet Flag Leaves From the Fifth Month*

Last Saturday 13th April, 2013, I took this photograph of a beautiful magnolia tree outside Queen's University, Belfast.

[214] *A Well-scented Robe*

At the moment, May 2nd 2013, our Zen teacher is here. He brought us beautiful incense from San Francisco Zen Centre. I was busy today but I still made the time to go the Zen Centre this morning. Paul is teaching a Zen koan class. Today we were in dyads and we had to ask our partner the following question, 'What does doing the right thing mean for you?' and your partner would reply, 'respond appropriately.'

[215] *On a Bright Moonlit Night*

During the Retreat at Benburb, I took a few photographs of the full moon. When I was there, I noticed the sign, 'Ghost Hunter's Breakfast.' I was intrigued and when I made inquiries, one of the staff told me that a group of ghost hunters were staying in the priory and they had their cameras with them. Apparently the ghosts or spirits stroll around the clock tower.

[216] *Things That Should be Big*

I agree with Sei, when she writes that cherry blossom petals should be big. These are the cherry blossom trees at Benburb, April 2013.

[217] *Things That Should be Small*

I think groups should be small. I do not like teaching big groups. It is a nightmare keeping up with the photocopying. I wrote a poem recently which was published by Community Arts Partnership, 'A Moment in Time '

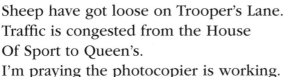

It's Friday 23rd November
    2012
I'm on the M5 heading to
    the College.
Sheep have got loose on Trooper's Lane.
Traffic is congested from the House
Of Sport to Queen's.
I'm praying the photocopier is working.

When I'm not having a panic attack about
The photocopier and the potential disaster
Of not having the required resources
I flick on the radio:
Sierra Leone's Koroma is re-elected
Iran slams Turkey's missile request,
Man dies in Gaza border shooting.

Kirsty Young's castaway
Is John Lloyd. He brought us *Spitting Image,
Not the Nine O'Clock News*, and *Blackadder.*
He talks openly about missed opportunities,
Roads not taken and multiple sackings.

His advice: there are starters and finishers,
And that's the great divide.

I arrive at the College.
What a relief, the copier is
Working but why is there a
Queue?

My advice: There are organised
People, and disorganised people,
And that's the great divide.

[218] *Things a House Should Have*
I would love more shelves for my books. I would like patio doors and a garden.

But I am happy with my home. I have lots of space. I like the rose on the ceiling, and the cornicing. In my hall there are two angel features. They are beautiful.

[219] *On Your Way Somewhere*
This is an amusing entry when Sei gets annoyed when her curiosity cannot be satisfied. I was very inspired to write poetry on the night of the full moon. We are not supposed to write while we are on a silent retreat, so I took a few photographs instead.

[220] *It Irritates me More Than Anything*
Sometimes queues irritate me more than anything. I hate wasting time queuing.

[221] *I Heard People Saying There'd been a Man in the Long Room who had no Business Being There*
This entry proves how claustrophobic the enclosed world of the Imperial Court was. I am just after listening to a discussion on The Ulster Hall, Belfast with its great acoustics. So many people including the Dalai Lama and the Reverend Ian Paisley have spoken there. There was an item about Nikolai Demidenko who

was playing Grieg's *Piano Concerto* and the conductor was as Estonian called Olari Elts.

[222] *When Her Majesty Was in the Sanjo Palace*
This intimate exchange between Her Majesty and Sei under-lines the high aesthetic that prevailed in court. I have a friend called Maura, who always lays out the table beautifully in the Zen Centre and puts beautiful flowers and cloths on the altar.

[223] *When the Nurse Taifu Went off to Hyoga*
Again this gift of the fan shows the sophistication of this cultured society.

[224] *Once When I was in Retreat at Kiyomizu Temple*
I particularly relish the notion of Sei writing her response to Her Majesty on a violet lotus petal. I wonder what she would have made of Facebook and Twitter, and the world of instant messaging. Surely we can learn something from this culture of cleverness and erudition.

[225] *Posting Stations*
Posting stations, known as shukuba or shukueki were towns where weary travellers could break their journey and have a rest. They were common in the Nara and Heian periods when goods were transported by horseback.

[226] *Shrines*
Shrines are places that are regarded as holy because some saint worked a miracle there or there was an apparition. There is a famous shrine in Lourdes which celebrates Mary's appear-ances to Bernadette, a poor village girl. I made a pilgrimage there a few years ago. People criticise it for all the religious memorabilia on sale in the little side streets, but I could see past the bric-a-brac, rows of Lourdes rosary beads, chains, crosses,

bottles of Lourdes water and other souvenirs to a beautiful spot where a holy lady appeared to a bare-footed child and revealed that she was the Immaculate Conception.

[227] *The Ichijo Palace Went by the Name of 'The Temporary Palace*

Sei conjures up a wonderful scene where His Majesty and his tutor are playing the flute.

[228] *Among the People Who Show You*

Sei shows her admiration for people who rise up in the world by receiving a promotion. I am quite ambitious myself and I do seek opportunities to promote my work. Recently I read some guidance some Paul Muldoon where he said that a writer should not worry about becoming rich and famous but rather should concentrate on receiving their gifts and listening to their inner voice. This advice helped me as I get anxious that my work will not be recognised.

[229] *It's Lovely to See a Day When the When the Snow Lies Thick*

I admire Sei's snow aesthetic. I kept this mini-journal during and after a recent snow event:

> Like ink wells spilt on the snow, the thaw came after ten days. Water dripped off the roof of the bus shelter outside St Malachy's on the Antrim Road. The snow re-treated to the edges leaving a white rectangular ridge around the perimeter. Big chunks withdrew to the side of the road outside Carryduff and in a few days began to resemble pieces of obsidian. One piece looked jagged like a piece of diabolical pavlova. One piece looked like a man kneeling before the executioner's block. It reminded me of the scene in *Skyfall* where Javier kneels before

Bond. One obnoxious piece jutted out on to the road and cried big inky tears. Cars were actually having to pull out to get past this lachrymose blob, which had not the ingenuity to shape itself into a recognisable form.

Little snow clumps had hatched out and were hiding under the cypress tree in Joyce's garden in Mountsandel, Coleraine. The little crocuses seemed to be in cahoots with them and were in no hurry to betray them.

Its abominable grip had not slackened on the Drumclig Road where walls of snow flanked the road. Driving through at 5pm I felt it had formed a guard of honour for my benefit. The crows seemed unperturbed as they dropped down to their evening abodes. Crows are never in crisis mode. One of the hedges looked like a crown of thorns.

Was the snow on the ground the writing on the wall? The melting sculptures bore no resemblance to the hot cross buns I made this Easter…neat little parcels of dough rolled into 12 pieces on a lightly floured board, and arranged on a baking tray lined with parchment.

Half for you and half for me
Between us goodwill shall be

A little piece of snow at the side of the road looked like a flattened seal.

[230] *It is Also Charming to Witness*
I always wonder how anyone can do night duty. My sleep is so precious to me. I think I would get ill if I had to stay awake all night.

[231] *Hills*

The Cave Hill is my favourite hill. There are so many legends associated with it, which include highwaymen, United Irishmen and the profile of the sleeping giant which may have inspired Jonathan Swift's to write *Gulliver's Travels*.

[232] *Things That Fall*

There were hailstones today. (Saturday, 11th May 2013) I stopped at Tesco's on the Antrim Road buy some olive oil. I cooked green lentils and I found a recipe for them which involved olive oil, lemon juice, sun blushed tomatoes and halloumi cheese and not forgetting red onion. Needless to say, there were no sun blushed tomatoes. Tesco's used to be called Stewarts. I should have gone to ASDA.

[233] *Kinds of Sun*

After getting soaked this morning, I headed out again to the Waterworks park and the sun was making an appearance. I also like how it shone on the St Anne's Cathedral Spire of Hope yesterday evening as I was looking out before the meditation session.

[234] *Kinds of Moon*

My dharma name is Ocean Moon. There was a perfect half-moon on the 5th March 2013. It was like a silver segment hanging in the sky. There was a veil of mist in front of it.

[235] *Stars*

I heard the expression dead stars the other day. In Sean O'Casey's *Juno and the Paycock*, this interchange takes place:

> *Boyle: An' as it blowed an'blowed, I ofen looked up at the sky an'assed meself the question-what is the stars, what is the stars?*

Joxer: Ah, that's the question, that's the question- what is the stars?

Boyle: An'then, I'd have another look, an' I'd ass meself-what is the moon?

Joxer: Ah, that's the question, that's the question- what is the moon, what is the moon?

[236] *Clouds*

This entry is a sky/life journal I jotted down February to April 2013:

Weather

25/02/13 8.22am

It was minus one degree centigrade this morning. I was walking towards the car and I realised I would have to go back and get water to clear the windscreen. Sitting on the train to Coleraine, I can see rushes poking out of the white fields and little streams. The sun is rising.

I see horses in the field just as we were approaching Ballymoney. A woman in a grey poncho shields her eyes with her hand as she looks across the platform. A boy with his hands dug into his pockets. A young student with a bag strung across his shoulders climbs the steps that lead to the bridge over the track. A woman is carrying a blue bag with ladybirds on it.

A man is smoking a cigarette. Three women, all with suitcases with wheels are standing on the platform like witches out of *Macbeth*. Suddenly a train has pulled in and has scooped away the passengers on the other side like some alien spaceship. Trees cast shadows across the fields.

6/3/13

The sky is cloudy today. It rained earlier. I am sitting in the car park outside Ballymena College. A dog is pacing round and round its small backyard. It is as trapped as me. The hedge spar-rows busy themselves in the bushes. A robin set on top of a branch and looked about like the lord mayor. Two thrushes root among the leaves at the foot of the trees.

11/03/13

It was minus two degrees this morning. But it was quite clear...I stood at my kitchen sink in Kansas Avenue and had the sensation that the heavy coat of winter was slipping off. I saw pigeons perched on the roofs of Cedar Avenue, like gloomy sentinels. Driving down Kansas, the sun was coming up over Glandore Avenue, and I could see Samson and Goliath in the Titanic Quarter jutting out like the city's conscience. Years ago 18,000 men in cloth caps and

I met this beautiful Irish wolfhound in the grounds of Queen's University

rough working clothes, piece in hand, would have been crossing Queen's Bridge, ready to hammer thousands of rivets into the ships, maybe even the doomed Titanic. Driving down Limestone Road, I noticed white greyish smoke pouring out of a factory chimney, as if trying to merge with the grey clouds in the sky. After parking the car in York Street Station I ascended the steps to the station, noticing a clump of dignified daffodils on the way. I heard on the news that we need to develop new antibiotics. Also that the bus driver in the Indian rape case has killed himself in prison. Savita's last words to her mother were 'I hope they burn.' I wanted to say the brute deserved to die and I was finding it hard to feel compassion for him. The Huhnes will be sentenced today. She was seen at the weekend buying black bin liners and hair dye. Have the media not punished these people enough?

Weather

The setting sun gives a pink tinge to the sky as I look out of the classroom in Magherafelt College. Traffic is leaving and heading to Cookstown. I see the tailights. A big ASDA truck with its familiar green and white lettering rumbles along. I see a garage on the right.

There are street lights which emit an orange light. They are curved at the top. Some traffic is coming into the town. Tonight my ESOL students are doing a practice paper. I explained that you do not count sheeps but sheep. I also explain what 'annoyed' meant; also what 'pricey' meant, what 'hard up' meant, what 'out of work meant, and what a 'slap-up meal' meant?

We had a laugh in the English class this evening. One of the students pointed out that my blouse was inside out. Can you believe that?

15/03/13

Beware the Ides of March

Driving down to the Zen Centre, seagulls circled like planes around Atlantic Avenue.

The sky was blue as I drove towards the Templepatrick turn off. There were a few clouds...one big dark cloud which loomed over the sky like King Kong over the Empire State Building.

Except instead of fur, it was made of billowy smoke. I felt it might reach out and catch me.

Self-opinionated magpies with white breasts and white tipped wings were off on some vital mission. Crows scrounged around for twigs for their high rise nests. A solitary blackbird scurried under the fir tree outside Antrim Day Centre like a pedestrian running for shelter in a storm.

Driving back from Antrim

A group of clouds looked like a big hand holding big lumps of candy floss in its palm. After I had driven for a few miles the big cloudy fingers became blurred and the candy floss dissipated. I had the feeling that this mirrored my energy as after a peripatetic week round the college campuses I was like a punctured tyre. Or maybe a slow puncturing tyre...would I have enough puff to get back to Belfast?

At last it is nine degrees Celsius.

15/04/13
On train...just leaving Ballymoney.
There are white vapourish
clouds drifting across the sky.
Benefit capping starts today.
There was a rehearsal for
Mrs T's funeral last night.
Soldiers and sailors gathered
to rehearse the ceremony.

16/04/13
Winds 50 miles per hour at north coast.

17/04/13
Clouds gaseous, like
Wisps trailing across the sky
in the direction of Donegore.
One cloud looked like a
Turtle with a grey back
And white head.

18/04/13
Cloudscape grey blue
Wispish
One cloud looked like a foetus.

22/04/13
Sky looks like a big grey dome.

24/04/13
Bird chirping outside
Chairs creaking upstairs
As a class re-configures itself

The sky is grey. It is a soft evening.
I can see Rathcooole flats outside Room
C21 in Newtownabbey, also a church
Now and again a magpie flits past showing off its smart black
    and white cape.
I'm in Gestalt class
I'm trying to be experiential
But failing miserably
I just want to go home
And lie down for a week
Perls would be appalled
At me.

As far as connection goes, I'm
Chicken shit level.

[237] *Things That Create a Disturbance*
A sudden loud bang or noise. I think loud noises would disturb me the most.

[238] *Slovenly Looking Things*
I am not a judgemental person but I suppose I do like a certain amount of order in my life. I am just after googling the term 'slovenly' and I have come across this statistic:

> Sixty per cent of us helped someone out in the last month – compared to the average across all the countries of 39 per cent but we are the second slovenliest nation – spending just one and a half hours on housework, compared to the OECD average of two hours and eight minutes. But at least we weren't as bad as the Koreans, who do just one hour and nineteen minutes.[12]

[239] *People of Rough Speech*
I have heard the following words mispronounced in Coleraine over the last few years:

Ketch for catch
Tap for top
Waher, for water
Wrang for wrong
Drap for drop
Dour for door
Beg for bag
Oul for old

Coul for cold
Move oar for move over
Lave for leave
Hoult of me for hold of me
No harm in a bit of carry on
Sowl for sell
Beck for back
Pecket for packet
Toop for tea
Houl for hold
Hersel for herself
hissel for himself
I hay for I have
Awl for all
Boxc for box
Tae for tea

Impect for impact
I hidda mine to go down and pay for this
Weemen for women

[240] *People Who Are Smug and Cocky*
People who think they have it all…money, power and status.
These things can be taken from us at the drop of a hat.

[241] *Things That Just Keep Passing By*
The time…it's the 19th May 2013 and I can remember vividly
sitting in my front room in Kansas Avenue on Xmas day 2012.
Can five months have gone by so quickly?

[242] *Things That No One Notices*
Bluebells. I noticed a little clump outside the Post Script café,
Antrim Road, the other day.

[243] *I Particularly Despise People Who Express Themselves Poorly in Writing*

As an English teacher and creative writing tutor, I teach essay writing, fiction, and poetry. I did a really interesting exercise, which I found in David Morley's *Cambridge Book of Creative Writing* in Queen's in the third term. Morley wrote about Raymond Queneau's *Exercises in Style* which consists of the re-telling of a simple tale 99 times. He also mentioned Queneau's Oulipo, a group of experimental writers that included Italo Calvino, George Perec and Harry Mathews. The story concerns a narrator who witnesses an altercation between two men on the 'S' bus. Later in the same day, he sees one of the men at the Gare St-Lazare who lost a button, getting a lecture advice on how to sew it back on. The exercises are similar to Erasmus' *Copia: Foundations of the Abundant Style,* 1512.

This is a new version, *Cyberpunk,* by Jonathan Lethem:

He jacked the passengerbus mainframe, but some interface residue snizzled up his data stream slightly, reducing optic input to a distracting 5-D glance at an idiot avatar with a comically distorted head-to-shoulders assembly and spex-ribbon ringing his head like a doll's bow. It more than figured that 68Gasm would parachute him into the passenger-grid unannounced; typical sense of humor for a four-hour subroutine maxed out of spare giggs. Even while observing this, Queneau detected a noisy lattice overlay just beneath the horizon of his optics, the scuffling of one infoshoe against another, vying to divvy the limited floorgrid. He took little notice. Putting aside static one avatar might offload to another, the scuffle was merely a generic output of the overlay.

Abruptly now he veered: in a segue that could have been lightyears or a pixel blink, he found himself exo-gloved into the Saint-Lazare spectrum, the brink of the matter at hand. These pitches always nauseated Queneau, no matter how inured he should be by now to the recursion-toxicity. *The button!* he screamed silently.[13]

[244] *Horrid Filthy Things*
That reminds me of Shakespeare's witches in *Macbeth* who were referred to as 'filthy hags'.

[245] *Terrifying Things*
Once my car got burnt outside my door. It was very stressful. Believe it or not, I was able to attend my meditation the next day. The 'Troubles' were horrific. Between 1969 and 1998, 3,600 people lost their lives and that does not include many others who were maimed. Not to mention the psychological damage.

[246] *Things That Give You Confidence*
Trying out a new thing and succeeding.

[247] *A Son-in-law is Brought In*
I read in the *Guardian* recently that baby boomers are the most lonely and unhappy people in the country because a lot of their marriages have broken down.

[248] *Being Disliked by Others*
I try not to worry about other people's opinions.

[249] *Men Have Most Unlikely and Peculiar Feelings*
There was a book published a few years ago called '*Men are From Mars, Women are From Venus*'.

[250] *Nothing is More Wonderful Than Sympathy*
Tea and sympathy, a friend who listens.

CHAPTER SEVEN:

Things of Splendour and Spectacle

[251] *I Really Cannot Understand People Who Get Angry*

Ecclesiastes 7:21 states the following:

Also take no heed unto all words that are spoken; lest thou hear thy servant curse thee.

This is good advice. Nobody wants to hear people gossiping about them. I wrote a short story on this theme:

She looked at Celia in her designer suit and her perfect slim figure. Once Celia told Julia a funny story about stopping on the Lisburn Road for a cream bun on a Friday evening and when she came out, she had a parking ticket. She was human after all; she made mistakes just like everyone else. She always liked to carry a coffee in one of those fancy 'to-go' mugs.

Julia had a group of female friends who labelled themselves as the 'corrosive viragoes'. They had some great stories to tell. The viragoes were always getting into trouble. Once John reported one of them maybe for using the Ballygowan filtered water for filling the kettle.

Those were the days!
Me at an Underwood typewriter The Cuan restaurant, Strangford, July 2013

At Christmas an office party always took place and there was a 'secret santa' thing introduced. Rory always go a bit carried away at the Xmas party and gave out about gerrymandering and the Brits. Sure he was just a mouth. And the Protestants in the office laughed it off. They were just as drunk as him

[252] *The Thing about Someone's Face*
They say the eye is the mirror of the soul. In a fashion conscious world, there is a burgeoning fashion industry.

It is said that Helen of Troy, who was abducted by Paris, was so beautiful that Greek troops manned 1,000 ships and went to war to win her back for Menelaus. Her face launched a 1,000 ships. In scene xiii in Marlowe's play *Faustus*, Faustus declares:

Faust. Was this the face that launched a thousand ships?
And burnt the topless towers of Ilium
Sweet Helen, make me immortal with a kiss
Her lips suck forth my soul; see where it flies!

[253] *Old-fashioned People Put on Their Gathered Trousers*
This is a humorous entry where Sei criticises the men fumbling with gathered trousers.

[254] *Once Towards the Middle of the Tenth Month*
I remember seeing stupas in a Buddhist monastery in Samye Ling in Eskdalemuir, Scotland. This is a definition that I find useful:

The Stupa represents Buddha's holy mind, Dharmakaya, and each part of the Stupa shows the path to Enlightenment. Building a Stupa is a very powerful way to purify negative karma and obscurations, and to accumulate extensive merit. In this way you can have realizations of the path to Enlightenment and be able to do perfect work to liberate suffering beings, who equal the sky, leading them to the peerless happiness of Enlightenment, which is the ultimate goal of our life.[14]

[255] *Captain Narinobu Was Wonderful at Distinguishing People's Voices*

I think the late Richard Burton had a wonderful voice. I read once that Elizabeth had not a brilliant voice.

His legs bestrid the ocean: his rear'd arm
Crested the world: his voice was propertied
As all the tuned spheres, and that to friends;
But when he meant to quail and shake the orb,
He was as rattling thunder. (*Antony and Cleopatra*)

[256] *No One had Sharper Ears than the Minister of the Treasury*

I have been told that I have acute hearing. I think it is important to listen to people and really attend to what they are saying.

[257] *Things That Give You Pleasure*

I bought some great books today. One of them, *Dream Power* by Dr Faraday, has an interesting piece on the Gestalt take on dreams:

Perls had no time for tracing back associations to some dubious infantile trauma, but concentrated like Jung, on discovering buried treasure within the personality...he focused his attention on actual behaviour in a group situation---facial expression, tone of voice, posture,

gesture, reactions to other members, and so on---in order to discover the 'holes' present in a person's present
personality.

As well as buying interesting books I love nature. I noticed
these little cygnets huddling beside their mother this
morning:

[258] *I Was Talking
With Some People in
Her Majesty's Presence*
Today was the hundredth
anniversary of the death of
Emily Wilding Davison, 4th
June 1913. A famous suffra-
gette, she was killed at the
Epsom Derby after throwing herself in front of Anmer, King
George's horse. I read a poem by P.B. Shelley called, 'To A
Skylark'.

Hail to thee, blithe Spirit
Bird thou never wert-
That from Heaven or near it
Pourest thy full heart
In profuse strains of unpremeditated art.

[259] *On the Twenty-First Day of the Second Month*
Sei describes a dedication ceremony in the Sakuzen Temple
of Hoko Palace. The creation of an artificial cherry tree shows
the lengths gone to evoke atmosphere in this period. Once again
Sei's sensibilities are compromised when she witness the vulgar
scramble for seats in the carriages.

Hyacinths in Botanic Gardens, Belfast

A whole bed of hyacinths beside
The palm house stole the show.

I could not quite describe the
Heady scent; was it Anais
Anais?

Zephyrus' mischief
destroyed
Hyakinthos

Apollo wept.
A hyacinth blossomed.

I read this beautiful poem by Muslihuddin Sadi, 13th century Persian poet:

If, of thy mortal goods, thou art bereft,
And from thy slender store two loaves
alone to thee are left,
Sell one & from the dole,
Buy Hyacinths to feed the soul.

I wrote this poem about the priory peacocks during the spring retreat 2013:

Priory Peacock

Weighted down by a vanity of plumage
I thought you were supposed to strut

Through the grounds, not scuttle off
In a huff as if in sudden fit of petty pique
Over some perceived slight or innuendo
Carting your iridescent tail like a jilted
Bride.

I thought you were supposed to be proud
Standing above the ducks and geese
So it's all lies, half truths, hearsay.

[260] *Venerable Things*

Venerate, comes the Latin, *venerari,* worship. Venerari comes from Veneris/Venus, the goddess of love. Venerate means to revere. The adjective venerable means 'worthy of reverence, hallowed by associations or are, an honorific prefix to the name of an archdeacon, or one in process of canonisation'. These words have loosed their moorings from their original Latin roots, but I think it's really important to revisit their origins.

This is a picture of my venerable teacher, Paul Haller, Roshi, and former abbot of San Francisco Zen Centre.

[261] *Songs*

When I visited Paris a few years ago, I remember people singing and dancing in the square. It was amazing. Our teacher was Miss McCabe. I loved singing in French.

Someday I would like to visit Avignon and dance on the bridge and sing this song.[15]

Sur le Pont d'Avignon
L'on y danse, l'on y danse
Sur le Pont d'Avignon
L'on y danse tous en rond

On the bridge of Avignon
We all dance there, we all dance there
On the bridge of Avignon
We all dance there in a ring.

I also remember people singing and dancing in the square. It was amazing. As far as I can remember the song was called 'Frou, Frou':

The woman sometimes wears pants at home.
It's an established fact, I think, within the nuptial tie (the marital life).
But when she goes cycling in pants like a zouave,
This fact becomes more worrying,
and I to myself at that sight...

Frou-frou
Frou-frou
By her petticoat the woman troubles the man's soul
For surely the woman entices above all, with her gentle frou-frou.

I took this picture of a couple dancing outside Castle Court in Belfast. It was wonderful Belfast being stable enough to have a couple dancing in the street rather than diving for cover after a bomb warning. I am so sorry for those who are not able for one reason or another are incapable of celebrating how far we

have come. Senator Mitchell's son commented that Stormont was boring. Senator Mitchell said boring is good, bombing is bad.

This is another picture of a city teaming with life. It is me along with my teacher Paul Haller in the Cathedral Quarter in 2010. Paul had just finished teaching a mindfulness workshop at Antrim

Terracotta Warriors

The Warriors of Xi'an China are curren the grounds of Belfast City Hall, as part of the One World Creative programme. These imperial figures were fashioned as a replicate army to guard Qin Shi Huang, the First Emperor of China. The imperial figures form an integral part of Chinese history and were originally commissioned by the First Emperor of China, Qin Shi Huang. Pamela Lee said: 'We've had a fabulous response. We host free events so everyone can join in.' It is hoped that the warriors will engender a notion of shared space.

[262] *Gathered Trousers*

My grandmother, who was born around 1882, never wore trousers. She used to tell us that she knew a woman who was so virtuous that she never looked in a mirror. She said make-up was sinful and as for mini-skirts, she just abhorred them. A couple kissing on the TV was completely anathema. In fact she used to censor these scenes.

I think the image of 'trousers in the lapis lazuli blue of summer insects gives a sense of coolness' is picture-perfect. Recently I have been reading the Book of Isaiah from the Old Testament:

Afflicted city, lashed by storms and not comforted,
I will rebuild you with stones of turquoise
your foundations with lapis lazuli. (54:11)

Belfast, afflicted city
Lashed by bombs
Not solaced.

Let us rebuild you
With Latin American
Dance steps

Let us lay your
Foundations with
Sapphire, onyx
Topaz, quartz.

[263] *Hunting Costumes*
This entry reminds me of a witty quote from Oscar Wilde where he described the English fox hunter in pursuit of the fox as the 'unspeakable in pursuit of the inedible'.

[264] *Shifts*
In January 1907, a line from Synge's *Playboy of the Western World* 'a drift of females standing in their shifts' caused riots as the reference to shifts (female undergarments) was considered immoral.

[265] *Formal Train Robes*

I noticed these pretty First Communion dresses in Jean Millar's bridal salon in Royal Avenue. When I made my first com-

munion in 1962 I borrowed my cousin's dress, walked out the lane from my house and no one even took my photograph. Holy Communion dresses are like wedding dresses. Children are dressed up like brides, and are taken out for meals.

I met these two Shaolin Monks at the Tom Duffy Circus in Antrim. They were wearing robes.

[266] *Fan Ribs*

I found this interesting little piece about fans:

> The fan has many different uses. It is used as a symbol of elegance, and also as a language.., and to refresh us when we feel hot. During many years the fan served to transmit feelings and hidden passions. The postures and looks made possible a new way of expression taking care of showing women's femininity.[16]

[267] *Cypress Fans*

Fans have a specific terminology for each of their components:
País: textile.

varillas (ribs): wood that can be painted or fret-worked.
caberas: first and last ribs thicker than the others.
calado (fretwork): holes made in the ribs.
abanico (fan): the assembly or the named elements.[17]

[268] *Deities*

As a practising Catholic, I am monotheistic.
Recently I have been reading the Book of Isaiah:[18]

[10] You are my witnesses," declares the Lord,
"and my servant whom I have chosen,
so that you may know and believe me
and understand that I am he.
Before me no god was formed,
nor will there be one after me.
I, even I, am the Lord,
and apart from me there is no saviour.
[12] I have revealed and saved and proclaimed—
I, and not some foreign god among you.
You are my witnesses," declares the Lord, "that I am God.
[13] Yes, and from ancient days I am he.
No one can deliver out of my hand.
When I act, who can reverse it?"

[269] *Promontories*

Portrush means promontory port.

[270] *Huts*

This is a verse from Isaiah 1.8:
And the daughter of Zion is left as a booth in a vineyard, as
a hut in a garden of cucumbers, as a besieged city. (King James
Bible 2003)

[271] *The Calling of the Night Watch is a Wonderful Thing*
I will make a found poem from the words in this wonderful entry:

I love to listen to the clatter
Watchmen dragging their feet
The night is starry, the snow deep
A distant voice cries out
Third quarter
Hour of the Ox

Fourth quarter
Hour of the Rat
Country people
Cry, Ox eight strikes
Rat nine strikes

[272] *At Noon on a Beautiful Sunny Day*
This is the summer solstice. The weather has been quite sunny.

[273] *Captain Narinobu*
I agree with Sei's comment that rain is depressing.

[274] *You Have a Lover Who Always Sends You a Next Morning Poem*
These days, lovers would be more inclined to send a text or an email. I wrote this poem after reading Wislawa Szymborska's 'Possibilities'.

I prefer the road not taken
I prefer quiet men
I prefer profiteroles

I prefer tea
I prefer wells to reservoirs
Especially holy wells with
Miraculous cures
I prefer people to plants
I prefer pancake Tuesday
To Ash Wednesday
I prefer Petrarch because he wrote
366 sonnets to a woman he barely
Knew and could never possess.

[275] *Things of Splendour and Spectacle*
I think the cranes, Samson and Goliath in the Titanic Quarter,
are spectacular:

I was at an end of term art exhibition in the Northern Regional
College recently and I used
Photobooth from my IPad to take
this photo from one of the pieces
exhibited.

[276] *When There are Great Thunderclaps*
One of the cars card from my I
Ching deck states the 'the authority of a great leader should rouse
people like thunder.'

[277] *The Kongenroku Screen is a Fascinating Thing*
I can image Sei sitting behind her screen, composing a haiku
in response to some love letter she has received from an ad-
mirer. In the Heian period, murals, scrolls, folding screens and
sliding doors were popular in Japanese aristocratic houses.

[278] *A Seasonal Directional Taboo*

When I visited Japan I noticed Shinto shrines. These shrines are not like our western cathedrals, huge and ornate; rather they are built in harmony with nature, perhaps set in a quiet wooded area. They are places for offering prayers to the Kami, for guidance and protection.

I read this charming (literally) book in the McClay Library at Queen's University: *A New Critical History of Old English Lit.* Stanley B. Greenfield and Daniel G. Calder.

Against a Wen
Blickling Homilies

Charms against bees swarming
Bald's Leechbook and Lacnunga

Against bees swarming, take earth, cast it with your right
hand under your right foot, and say:
I catch it under foot, I have found it.
Lo, earth has power against all creatures,
and against malice and against neglect,
and against the mighty tongue of man (i.e., an evil spell).
(Whereupon cast sand over them, when they swarm and say:)
Settle down, victory-women, sink to earth,
never be wild and fly to the woods.
Be as mindful of my welfare
as is each man of eating and home.

Charm against storms brewing
Against storms brewing, cast it with your left
hand and say:
Lo Neptune fierce God of the sea
Take pity on me, Calm the storm,

Caress the waves, which are
mocking us like accursed dancers
settle the foam
Be mindful of our ship, guide
us safely to land
Save us from sea-dragons
sea monsters
Sea snakes, marvels and monsters.

[279] *The Snow was Piled High*
This is a view of St Anne's Cathedral, Donegall Street, Belfast,
January 2013.

[280] *The Little Boy Employed by the Yin-Yang Masters is Terribly Clever*
I consult the I Ching occasionally.

[281] *In the Third Month, I Left the Court*
Sei commits a grave error for her inappropriate use of the word 'unbearable' in her message to the empress. Such were the social linguistic nuances of the time.

[282] *On the Twenty-Fourth Day of the Twelfth Month*
The full moon at Benburb April 2013.

[283] *When Gentlewomen in the Palace Leave*
Sei asks if it is wrong to be fascinated by people in high ranking positions. Nowadays there is a voracious appetite for celebrity gossip. The new royalty is the film stars and the pop

stars. Sometimes when I read a women's magazine in the hair-dressing salon I have to ask the stylist who is this person or who is that actor. I had never heard of Kim Kardashian. I jotted down a few items that I read in the Salon:

Fashion
London Fashion Week
Mick Jagger liked a clar-
    et-coloured frock-coat
    twinkling with irides-
    cent gold threads came
    down the catwalk.

Jan Moir:
Clouds of pastel cashmere
Tie-silks and diamonds

Mila Kunis

Esquire's sexiest woman alive
Ranked third in Maxim Hot 100
Women List

Looking Puffy
And red, she
Leaves a London
Hotel without makeup
No slap on
Hair scraped back in a bun
When she hits the red carpet

She needs Clarin's Beauty Flash Balm
To revive her skin

She needs Touche Éclat
For under the eyes
She needs her eyebrows shaped
She needs her cheek defined
She needs her nose contoured with
Clever shading
She needs black eyeliner
On her upper and lower eyeline

20 ways to fake a facelift/Kim Jones
Saggy neck saviours
Chisel your cheekbones
Lightening and tightening primers

Sugar coated
Spring's pastel palette in a candy shop array
of colours, bubblegum pink, powder blue, peppermint
And parma violet

Kate Moss
Hunter Wellies,
J Brand flared jeans
Skinny Sass and Bide jeans
Balenciaga Lariat bag
Vuitton leopard scarf
Monkey fur
Buckled Vivienne Westwood boot

Modelling deals
With Rimmel
St Tropez
Kerastase.

[284] *Things That Imitate*

I did a Google search and came up with a website, entitled 'Ten Ways to Imitate 'A' Lister Bloggers':

If you found this tip helpful… be consistent – Come what may you won't fail in posting daily. If you do, think of Daniel from Dailyblogtips, he has 12 drafts ready at any given moment of time.

[285] *Things One Must be Wary Of*

I think it's best not to agree to something too readily. I usually agree without checking my diary and basically I keep a mind diary and sometimes it lets me down.

[286] *A Certain Officer of the Right Gate Watch*

This excerpt reminds me of Synge's *Playboy of the Western World* where the protagonist is Christy Mahon. The barmaid Pegeen Mike falls madly in love with him. However it transpires that Mr Mahon Senior survived his son's murderous attack and seeks him out. After his cover is blown, she laments. 'I have lost my only playboy of the western world.' Conall Morrison directed a production of the play in the rebuilt Lyric Theatre in September 2012.

[287] *The Mother of the Ohara Gentleman*

The lotus is a metaphor for enlightenment. Like the lotus, we dwell in the realms of mud and dark water, yet through persistent practice, enlightenment will come.

[288] *The Letter Narihira's Mother the Princess Sent Him*

Sei is able to access a poetic sensibility that is enviable.

[289] *It's Terribly Depressing to Discover*

Sei betrays her snobbery as she refers to a 'worthless person'.

[290] *If a Mere Common Woman*
Again Sei's references are so un- PC.

[291] *The Officers of the Left and Right Gate Watch*
Sei is right to disapprove of these sordid goings on.

[292] *Grand Counsellor Korechika Presented Himself One Day*
Imagine if our First or Deputy First Minister delivered a talk on Chinese poetry. Last week the G8 came to Fermanagh. It is true Obama did quote W.B.Yeats and Seamus Heaney. He did not quote any Irish women's poetry. So disappointing! I took this photo from a TV bulletin:

Wurden ist Angela?

[293] *I Was Sitting One Day with Bishop Ryuen's Nurse Mama*
Bishop Donal McKeown gave a homily at the Clonard Novena on Sunday, 23rd June 2013

[294] *There was a Man Whose Mother Dies*
This is an excerpt from a story I wrote about the death of my mother in 1961:

Something didn't seem right! One minute Carmel and Joan were playing in the yard and the next, Agnes their older sister was calling them into the house. Carmel hated her play being interrupted, as it meant rosary and then bed. There was usually some reason to delay the grim order to return to the house, but today, she went along with. the demand and went back in. And then a really odd thing happened. Her uncle, Patrick was in the kitchen and everyone knew he was a quiet reclusive man who rarely made social calls. The next thing she remembered, everyone was kneeling down and Uncle Patrick was giving out a decade of the rosary. By the time he had given out the all the five sorrowful decades, he began, "Hail, Holy Queen, Mother of mercy, our life, our sweetness and our hope. To thee do we cry, poor banished children of Eve." Carmel noticed that at these words some of the other children were crying and she began to cry too. Grownups seemed upset but nobody said exactly what had happened. Just that there was clear feeling that things weren't right. And where was mammy?

[295] *A Certain Gentlewoman was Courted by the Governor of Totomi's Son*
The newspapers and magazines seem to thrive on the love affairs of the rich and famous. Personally I prefer to read about politics.

[296] *Stealing and Illicit Conversation with Someone*
Forbidden fruit tastes sweet. In this world of 24 hour surveillance could anyone dare have an illicit affair?

[297] *Can it be True?*
I have enjoyed this journey, reflecting on my own concerns through the prism of Sei's Shōnagon's *Pillow Book*.

Endnotes

1 http://japanracing.jp/_news2011/110930-04.html

2 http://www.sportingpost.co.za/2011/10/19/frontpage/vive-la-france

3 http://en.wikipedia.org/wiki/List_of_koans_by_Yunmen_Wenyan

4 http://www.economist.com/blogs/bagehot

5 http://www.sacred-texts.com/shi/hvj/hvj028.htm

6 http://blogs.goddard.edu/pitkin/blog

7 http://groups.yahoo.com/group/translatinghaiku/message/2025

8 Gergana Ivanova. Women's In-jokes in Heian Japan: *Makura no soshi* http://www.tru.ca/jsac2006/pdf/jsac2006_proceedings_ivanova_g_manuscript.Pdf (Accessed 13/06/12)

9 Claire M. Tylee, Elaine Turner and Agnes Cardinal, eds. *War Plays by Women: An International Anthology* (London: Routledge, 1999) 1.

10 Sigmund Freud. *Group Psychology and the Analysis of the Ego*, trans., ed., James Strachey. London: The Hogarth Press, 1967

11 http://www.irishpage.com/poems/spring.htm

12 http://www.thejournal.ie/irish-people-kind-but-slovenly-survey-120253-Apr2011

13 http://therumpus.net/2013/01/exercises-in-style/

14 http://www.stupa.org/stupas.htm

15 http://en.wikipedia.org/wiki/Sur_le_Pont_d'Avignon

16 http://www.flamencoexport.com/flamenco-best-sellers/fans.html

17 http://www.flamencoexport.com/flamenco-best-sellers/fans.html

18 http://www.biblegateway.com

Printed in Great Britain
by Amazon